FTCE Educational Media Specialist PK-12
Teacher Certification Exam

By: Sharon Wynne, M.S.
Southern Connecticut State University

"And, while there's no reason yet to panic, I think it's only prudent that we make preparations to panic."

XAMonline, INC.
Boston

XAMonline, Inc.
21 Orient Ave.
Melrose, MA 02176
Toll Free 1-800-509-4128
Email: info@xamonline.com
Web www.xamonline.com
Fax: 1-781-662-9268

Library of Congress Cataloging-in-Publication Data

Wynne, Sharon A.
    Educational Media Specialist PK-12: Teacher Certification / Sharon A. Wynne. -2nd ed.
    ISBN 978-1-58197-578-9
    1. Educational Media Specialist PK-12.   2. Study Guides.   3. FTCE
    4. Teachers' Certification & Licensure.   5. Careers

Disclaimer:
The opinions expressed in this publication are the sole works of XAMonline and were created independently from the National Education Association, Educational Testing Service, or any State Department of Education, National Evaluation Systems or other testing affiliates.

Between the time of publication and printing, state specific standards as well as testing formats and website information may change that is not included in part or in whole within this product. Sample test questions are developed by XAMonline and reflect similar content as on real tests; however, they are not former tests. XAMonline assembles content that aligns with state standards but makes no claims nor guarantees teacher candidates a passing score. Numerical scores are determined by testing companies such as NES or ETS and then are compared with individual state standards. A passing score varies from state to state.

Printed in the United States of America   œ-1

FTCE: Educational Media Specialist PK-12
ISBN: 978-1-58197-578-9

Table of Contents

Great Study and Testing Tips!

The focus of this study guide is to reinforce *what* you should study in order to prepare for the subject assessment, but equally important is *how* you study.

You can increase your chances of truly mastering the information by taking some simple, but effective steps.

Study Tips:

1. <u>Some foods aid the learning process</u>. Foods such as milk, nuts, seeds, rice and oats help your study efforts by releasing natural memory enhancers called CCKs (*cholecystokinin*) composed of *tryptophan*, *choline* and *phenylalanine*. All of these chemicals enhance the neurotransmitters associated with memory. Before studying, try a light, protein-rich meal of eggs, turkey and fish. All of these foods release the memory enhancing chemicals. The better the connections, the more you comprehend.

Likewise, before you take a test, stick to a light snack of energy boosting and relaxing foods. A glass of milk, a piece of fruit, or some peanuts all release various memory-boosting chemicals and help you to relax and focus on the subject at hand.

2. <u>Learn to take great notes</u>. A by-product of our modern culture is that we have grown accustomed to getting our information in short doses (i.e., TV news sound bites or USA Today style newspaper articles.)

Consequently, we've subconsciously trained ourselves to assimilate information better in <u>neat little packages</u>. If your notes are scrawled all over the paper, they fragment the flow of the information. Instead, strive for clarity. Newspapers use a standard format to achieve clarity. Your notes can be much clearer through use of proper formatting. A very effective format is called the *"Cornell Method."*

Take a sheet of lined, loose-leaf notebook paper and draw a line all the way down the paper about 1-2" from the left-hand edge.

Draw another line across the width of the paper about 1-2" up from the bottom. Repeat this process on the reverse side of the page.

Look at the highly effective result. You have ample room for notes, a left hand margin for special emphasis items or inserting supplementary data from the textbook, a large area at the bottom for a brief summary, and a little rectangular space for just about anything you want.

3. <u>Get the concept then the details.</u> Too often we focus on the details and don't gather an understanding of the concept. However, if you simply memorize only dates, places or names, you may well miss the whole point of the subject.

A key way to understand ideas is to put them in your own words. If you are working from a textbook, automatically summarize each paragraph in your mind. If you are outlining text, don't simply copy the author's words.

Instead, *rephrase* them in your own words. You remember your own thoughts and words much better than someone else's, and you subconsciously tend to associate the important details to the core concepts.

4. <u>Ask Why?</u> Pull apart written material paragraph by paragraph, and don't forget the captions under the illustrations.

Example: If the heading is "Stream Erosion", flip it around to read "Why do streams erode?" Then answer the questions.

If you train your mind to think in a series of questions and answers, not only will you learn more, but you will also lessen the test anxiety because you will be used to answering questions.

5. <u>Read for reinforcement and future needs</u>. Even if you only have 10 minutes, put your notes or a book in your hand. Your mind is similar to a computer; you have to input data in order to have it processed. *By reading, you are creating the neural connections for future retrieval.* The more times you read something, the more you reinforce the learning of ideas.

Even if you don't fully understand something on the first pass, *your mind stores much of the material for later recall.*

6. <u>Relax to learn. Go into exile.</u> Our bodies respond to an inner clock called biorhythms. Burning the midnight oil works well for some people, but not everyone.

If possible, set aside a particular place to study that is free of distractions. Shut off the television, cell phone and pager, and exile your friends and family during your study period.

If you really are bothered by silence, try background music. Light classical music at a low volume has been shown to aid in concentration over other types. Music that evokes pleasant emotions without lyrics is highly suggested. Try just about anything by Mozart. His work will relax you.

7. <u>Use arrows not highlighters</u>. At best, it's difficult to read a page full of yellow, pink, blue and green streaks. Try staring at a neon sign for a while and you'll soon see that the horde of colors obscure the message.

A quick note, a brief dash of color, an underline and an arrow pointing to a particular passage is much clearer than a horde of highlighted words.

8. <u>Budget your study time</u>. Although you shouldn't ignore any of the material, *allocate your available study time in the same ratio that topics may appear on the test.*

Testing Tips:

1. Get smart, play dumb. Don't read anything into the question. Don't make an assumption that the test writer is looking for something else than what is asked. Stick to the question as written and don't read extra things into it.

2. Read the question and all the choices *twice* before answering the question. You may miss something by not carefully reading, and then re-reading both the question and the answers.

If you really don't have a clue as to the right answer, leave it blank on the first time through. Go on to the other questions, as they may provide a clue as to how to answer the skipped questions.

If later on, you still can't answer the skipped ones . . . ***Guess.*** The only penalty for guessing is that you *might* get it wrong. Only one thing is certain; if you don't put anything down, you will get it wrong!

3. Turn the question into a statement. Look at the way the questions are worded. The syntax of the question usually provides a clue. Does it seem more familiar as a statement rather than as a question? Does it sound strange?

By turning a question into a statement, you may be able to spot if an answer sounds right, and it may also trigger memories of material you have read.

4. Look for hidden clues. It's actually very difficult to compose multiple-foil (choice) questions without giving away part of the answer in the options presented.

In most multiple-choice questions you can often readily eliminate one or two of the potential answers. This leaves you with only two real possibilities and automatically your odds go to Fifty-Fifty for very little work.

5. Trust your instincts. For every fact that you have read, you subconsciously retain something of that knowledge. On questions that you aren't really certain about, go with your basic instincts. **Your first impression on how to answer a question is usually correct.**

6. Mark your answers directly on the test booklet. Don't bother trying to fill in the optical scan sheet on the first pass through the test.

Just be very careful not to miss-mark your answers when you eventually transcribe them to the scan sheet.

7. Watch the clock! You have a set amount of time to answer the questions. Don't get bogged down trying to answer a single question at the expense of 10 questions you can more readily answer.

COMPETENCY 1.0   KNOWLEDGE OF THE ROLES OF THE LIBRARY MEDIA SPECIALIST

Skill 1.1   Identify the national guidelines that define the roles of the library media specialist.

National guidelines for school library media programs are provided in documents published by the American Association of School Librarians (AASL), a division of the American Library Association (ALA), and the Association for Educational Communications and Technology (AECT).

Information Power: Guidelines for School Library Media Programs, a collaboration of AASL/AECT, was published in 1988 to provide standardized national guidelines as a vision for school library media programs into the 21st century. The AASL/AECT Standards Writing Committee, along with contributors from public school districts, created a definitive work using standards that have been revised over the last thirty years.

These revised standards reflect the flexibility to manage today's library media centers and to direct centers into the future. The AASL/AECT mission objectives are echoed in President Bush's message during a speech at the 1991 White House Conference on Library and Information Services. The following is a summary of the guidelines culled from this speech and other publications, including *Information Power.*

1.   A democratic society guarantees the right of its populace to be well-informed. To this end, libraries and media centers of all kinds are the bastions of intellectual freedom.

2.   Literacy for all United States residents begins in the public school system. School readiness through access to ample media stimuli, facilities that provide physical access to materials across cultural and economic barriers, and a sound national goal, supported by legislative funding, will ensure that Americans can avail themselves of the information to which they are entitled.

3.   Americans will become more productive in the workplace by taking advantage of the technology offered in the Information Age. To support the school-to-work initiative, school library media centers must offer access and instruction in emerging technologies used in business and industry.

4. Collaborative efforts between schools, business, and community agencies will encourage life-long learning. *Information Power's* mission statement and the vision statements of many public schools specify life-long learning as their primary objective. Thus libraries, even in the schools, must become community centers, offering their materials and services to all segments of the public. Such open access also motivates school-aged students as they see adults continually seeking information and educational opportunities.

Note: Specific guidelines addressing personnel, budgets, resources and equipment, facilities, and leadership are included in discussions of performance indicators throughout this guide.

Skill 1.2 Identify the roles and responsibilities of the library media specialist as stated in the current national guidelines

AASL/AECT produces national guidelines covering the roles and responsibilities of the library media specialist. The following passage summarizes these principles.

The role of the school library media specialist is three-fold, as the specialist must facilitate the library media program, instruct students, and consult with faculty staff, and administrators.

The information specialist meets program needs by providing

1. Access to the facility and materials that is non-restrictive, whether economically, ethnically, or physically.
2. Communication to teachers, students, administrators and parents concerning new materials, services or technologies.
3. Efficient retrieval and information-sharing systems.

The teacher specialist is charged with the responsibilities of

1. Integrating information skills into the content curriculum.
2. Providing access to and instruction in the use of technology.
3. Planning jointly with classroom teachers the use and production of media appropriate to learner needs.
4. Using various instructional methods to provide staff development in policies, procedures, media production and technology use.

The instructional consultant uses her expertise to

1. Participate in curriculum development and assessment.
2. Assist teachers in acquiring information skills which they can incorporate into classroom instruction.
3. Design a scope and sequence of teaching information skills.
4. Provide leadership in the use and assessment of information technologies.

COMPETENCY 2.0   KNOWLEDGE OF THE INSTRUCTIONAL RESPONSIBILITIES OF THE LIBRARY MEDIA SPECIALIST

Skill 2.1   Identify information skills commonly found in a library media program's curriculum framework that should be integrated with the curriculum

This objective can be best achieved if there are existing scope and sequences in other curricular areas. Information skills, like any other content, should not be taught in isolation if they are to be retained and practiced. If no printed sequences exist, consult with teachers and/or team leaders about planning activities cooperatively to teach information and content skills concurrently.

Teaming with teachers will also meet their instructional objectives. Media specialists need to match resources to those objectives as well as suggest means for using media to demonstrate student skills' mastery. Achievement of the design of resource-based teaching units with supplemental or total involvement of the library media center resources and services satisfy levels 9 and 10 of Loertscher's eleven levels taxonomy. This assumes the active involvement of the school library media specialist in the total school program.

Finally, the self-esteem of students and teachers who learn information management skills is as significant as the information acquisition.

For tips to incorporate library media within school curriculum, please read the following suggested procedure.

Preparation:

1. Secure any printed scope and sequences from content areas.

2. Meet with team leaders or department chairs early in the year to plan an integrated, sequential program.

3. Attend department or grade-level meetings with specific time devoted to orienting teachers to available resources and services.

4. Plan best times to schedule orientations for entry level students and reviews for reinforcement.

Implementation:

1.	Conduct planned lessons. Distribute copies of objectives, activities, and resources.

2.	Review search strategies and challenge students to broaden their scope of resources used to locate information.

3.	Provide adequate time for students to carry out lesson activities using media center resources.

Evaluation:

1.	Solicit feedback from both students and teachers.

2.	Incorporate suggestions into lesson plans.

In addition to this suggested procedure, The International Society of Technology in Education has also developed National Educational Technology Standards (NETS) that outline information literacy skills. These standards can be presented to faculty as a means of encouragement in the collaborative process of integrating media into curriculum

The standards state that students should:
- have quick and easy access to information,
- learn to be critical evaluators of information,
- and be able to utilize information resourcefully.

**Skill 2.2	Identify the most appropriate media formats to meet a specific learning need**

Because each learning style benefits most from specific media formats, the following list pairs learning needs with recommended media formats. These pairings will assist a media specialist in promoting the development of strong media skills across the curriculum.

- **Auditory/ Linguistic** – video recordings, auditory recordings, interactive books on CD-ROM, music recordings, DVDs
- **Logical/ Mathematical** – graphing calculators, linear multimedia presentations, problem-solving software
- **Visual** – photos, illustrations, drawing software, artwork, color-coded ideas
- **Kinesthetic** – handheld devices (Palms or Alphasmart), virtual field trips, joysticks, other large motor skill computer devices

Skill 2.3   Identify information skills necessary for using electronic formats

"To be information literate, a person must be able to recognize when information is needed and have the ability to locate, evaluate, and use effectively the needed information" (ALA Presidential Committee on Information Literacy, Final Report, 1989).

As with a standard book, periodical, or paper search, the first step in using electronic formats is always to clarify ahead of time the information being sought and for what purpose. When assisting with a search, encourage teachers and students to ask these questions:

- "What information am I seeking and why?"
- "How broad a scope or how far back need I go in my search?"
- "What is *not* important for me to know about my topic?"
- "What is already known about my topic?"
- "Where can I find the information most readily?"

After answering these basic questions, the searcher will be prepared to use his or her skills to incorporate electronic resources into the search. Common information skills necessary when using electronic formats include the following:

- **Tool literacy** – a knowledge of the online or electronic tools (such as subscription databases, online searches, CD-ROM almanacs or encyclopedias) available to conduct information searches, as well as an understanding of which electronic formats are most likely to yield the results sought.

- **Search/Location Skills** – the ability to apply the appropriate search standards and terms in order to increase or narrow down one's search to a desirable yet thorough level

- **Evaluation Skills** – An understanding of how to compare, contrast, and analyze information and determine its usefulness to the task at hand

- **Validity Questioning** – The ability to spot and filter out (or at least make note of or account for) bias when collecting information, such as may be found in web sites purporting to share "common" information but in reality may be pushing a specific product, service, or viewpoint with which the site is affiliated. The ability to discriminate between fact and opinion is essential when using electronic (or any other) information based tool.

- **Organizing Information** – Electronic searches will often reveal an overabundance of information on any one topic, making it difficult for child, teacher, or media specialist to sort through the accumulation and home in on the pertinent/desired information. Learning to categorize, edit, and discard duplicate or unwanted information will expedite the process of searching for pertinent information.

—Tool Literacy
—Search/Location Skills
—Evaluation Skills
—Validity Questioning
—Organizing Information

COMPETENCY 3.0   KNOWLEDGE OF THE CURRICULUM CONSULTANT RESPONSIBILITIES OF THE LIBRARY MEDIA SPECIALIST

Skill 3.1   Identify methods of cooperative instructional planning

Instructional planning for the school library media specialist is the process of effectively integrating library skills instruction into the curriculum.

Methods of instructional planning:

1.   Identify content. Teachers create a list of instructional objectives for specific classes. Library media specialists, using state and local scope and sequence, prepare a list of objectives for teaching information skills.
2.   Specify learning objectives. Teachers and library media specialists working together should merge the list of objectives.
3.   Examine available resources.
4.   Determine instructional factors:
      a.   Learner styles.
      b.   Teaching techniques and teacher and library media specialist division of responsibilities in the lesson implementation.
      c.   Student groupings. Consider abilities and special needs.
5.   Pretest.
6.   Determine activities to meet objectives.
7.   Select specific resources and support agencies.
8.   Implement the unit.
9.   Evaluate.
10.   Revise the objectives and/or activities.

Skill 3.2   Identify methods for keeping abreast of changes in curriculum

Since the media specialist is responsible for incorporating information technology into school curriculum, media specialists should keep abreast of changes in this curriculum. Being an active member of the school's and district's curriculum and planning committees is the best way to stay current with local changes. Since many changes also occur on the state and national levels, media specialists must also be involved with state and national organizations.

At the state level, media specialists can participate in various educational associations specific to the populations they serve. For instance, the Florida Association for Media in Education (FAME) serves as an advocate for school libraries. State level curriculum committees also seek educators to help update standards.

Florida
Association for
Media in
Education

The Association for Supervision and Curriculum Development (ASCD) plays an important role in the shaping of the nation's curriculum efforts. Recognizing curriculum changes requires

1. Analysis of current literature and national or state legislation and guidelines.
2. Study of the existing school and district curriculum and its reflection of current standards and future trends.
3. Consultation with local and district curriculum planners and participation in workshops or programs that address curriculum change.

If a media specialist plans to be involved in the tracking and updating of curriculum, he or she must be willing to perform such responsibilities.

Skill 3.3   Identify resources that indicate trends and directions in education

Periodicals in the fields of library/information sciences and technology are excellent sources of education trends. These include:

- *Florida Media Quarterly,*

- *Media and Methods,*

- *Multi-Media Schools,*

- *New Media,*

- *Florida Technology in Education Quarterly,*

- *School Library Media Quarterly,*

- and *School Library Journal.*

The *School Library Media Annual*, published since 1983, has included a section on "Trends and Forecasts" in each edition. The American Library Association's website also keeps a current list of trends and issues.

In addition to these publications, state and national conferences include workshops and programs covering educational trends, curriculum change, and innovative ways to use new technologies.

Skill 3.4   Identify the components of an instructional planning process and the school library media specialist's role on the instructional planning team

Current research indicates that school library media specialists should become more involved in curriculum planning, both on school and district curriculum teams. Sometimes principals must be coaxed into including school library media professionals in curriculum planning because they occasionally forget that media professionals are technically teaching professionals. The school library media specialist must volunteer to participate and hope that the administration places a value on the contribution she or he has to offer. As a team member, the school library media specialist contributes by

1.   Advising of current trends and studies in curriculum design.
2.   Advising the school staff on the use of media and instructional techniques to meet learning objectives.
3.   Ensuring that a systematic approach to information skills instruction will be included in curriculum plans.
4.   Recommending media and technologies appropriate to particular subject matter and activities.

COMPETENCY 4.0   KNOWLEDGE OF METHODS FOR TEACHING STUDENTS INFORMATION LITERACY

Skill 4.1   Identify activities that can enhance students' developmental skills in reading, writing, viewing and listening

As students utilize library information resources, they develop information literacy skills that adhere to the various taxonomies of overall learning skills. To reinforce these learning skills, a library media specialist should encourage students to follow a series of suggested activities.

1.   **Recall** expects the ability to retell a story in proper sequence and to identify the characters and places where the events occur. School library media specialists can suggest titles of books, filmstrips or videotapes appropriate for each user's ability and interest. Young students can exhibit recall mastery by orally retelling the story, dramatizing the story through role play, and drawing pictures or making puppets of the characters. Mature students can develop a story board and create slides or videotapes of their own reenactment. PK-2 students should be expected to recall a list of instructions and act on them. Training them in the use of location, retrieval, and circulation procedures will enhance their listening skills so they can become productive media center users.

2.   **Comprehension**. Students in upper primary grades exhibit the ability to explain the main idea of a passage or the theme of a story. Reading, listening, and viewing can be enhanced by outlining the main points of a written passage, audiotape or record, and any of the visual media: filmstrips, slides, videotapes, laser disks. At this level, students can produce slides, transparencies, posters or models that demonstrate their understanding of the material. They can show the cause/effect relationship of happenings by discussing and practicing the behavioral procedures required to work cooperatively in the media center.

3. **Inference**. After reading a story or book, listening to a record or audiotape, or viewing a filmstrip or videotape, a middle school student should be able to interpret character actions, determine the logic of plot sequences, relate knowledge from the reading to real life, and infer information about characters from dialogue. They might predict a new course of action, were a given event to change. Some middle school and most high school students should be able to discuss inferences after reading, viewing, or listening to most media formats. Students at this point can learn to discriminate the appearance and function of various media formats and match them to appropriate learning activities. Students at this level may also be encouraged to study television production, photography or related media arts. Students may be planning and producing daily announcements via closed circuit television.

4. **Evaluation**. Secondary students now judge the quality and appropriateness of reading materials, making selections independently. They can be expected to assess the quality of the author's writing style, the effectiveness of character and plot development, the bias of the writer's/producer's presentation, and the appropriateness of the language used to convey information. Students at this level should master concentrated listening skills by taking study notes from printed matter, lectures, or audio-visual programs. Learning should not only result in written research papers but in audio-visual projects. Students should be taught design, production, and editing skills.

5. **Appreciation**. To be accomplished in varying degrees at every level is the ability to express an emotional response to subject matter or a reaction to the author's language or a film's theme or graphic detail. Younger students' reactions will be observable immediately, and requests for more of the same will keep the media specialist searching for similar materials. Older youngsters can be expected to write appraisals that incorporate evaluation and appreciation skills. Those with definite, vocal opinions may be encouraged to serve on the library media advisory committee.

Lower Level ↗
- Recall
- Comprehension
- Inference
- Evaluation
- Appreciation
Higher Level ↘

Skill 4.2   Identify activities that can develop students' critical thinking skills

Critical thinking skills are essential if students are to evaluate the information presented to them. A media specialist will introduce and develop student critical thinking skills, providing students the tools to question not only the assumptions of others, but their own ideas, thoughts, and established opinions as well.

Too many students prefer a passive absorption of information without questioning its origin, usefulness, bias or purpose. Without critical thinking skills, it's unlikely these students will have high retention of the material they learn.

Critical thinking skills develop from even the simplest of tasks set to students. Any assignment that asks children to make a choice or state an opinion is an exercise in critical thinking.

Encourage activities such as group discussion, summary writing, identifying the central idea or question in the topic studied, or drawing conclusions using supporting evidence. Encourage statements of opinion, assumptions, or observation. You will find students respond differently to instructional methods, which is why it's important to have a full arsenal of critical thinking skill activities available.

Work with the teachers to develop and coordinate ongoing critical thinking activities (such as having students research and then present both sides of a topic). Encourage the exploration of questions (stated at an age-appropriate level) such as "What do I think about this topic? Why? What more would I wish to learn? How did I arrive at my conclusion or observation?"

Such challenges to analyze and evaluation research materials will continue to foster the development of student critical thinking skills.

research + present both sides

• opinion
• assumptions
• observation

Skill 4.3 **Identify activities that demonstrate students have acquired reading, writing, viewing, listening and critical thinking skills**

Reading, writing, viewing, listening and critical thinking are independent and inseparable skills, as strength in one area leads to strength in the other areas. Consistency in practice and application will enhance and encourage these skills in children.

Activities that demonstrate students have acquired and are applying these skills include the following:

- Students exhibit curiosity and ask questions.
- Students are able to identify central themes and main ideas on a basic level.
- Students are able to separate fact from opinion.
- Students are able to write or articulate multiple sides of an argument.
- Students are able to summarize—verbally or in writing—information presented to them.
- Students question assumptions—whether their own or the author of a work.
- Students exhibit respect for and or curiosity about countering viewpoints.
- Students actively seek out additional information to support or question their knowledge of a topic.
- Students read for enjoyment.
- Students come to class prepared.
- Students ask pertinent questions.
- Students decipher—or try to decipher—unknown vocabulary terms from their context.
- Students reread or ask for clarification on what they don't understand.
- Students demonstrate age-appropriate writing skills in terms of outlining, organizing, drafting, and revision.

As students display these skills, the media specialist should challenge students to move beyond the basic levels of critical thinking when dealing with audio, video, or written samples.

Skill 4.4   Identify methods to evaluate the effectiveness of an activity used to develop reading, writing, listening, viewing, and critical thinking skills.

As a media specialist challenges students to develop their reading, writing, listening, viewing, and critical thinking skills, he or she must continually evaluate the effectiveness of the activities that provide these challenges. As a result, the media specialist can continue to hone these tasks as a means to provide a more effective learning experience for all involved. Here are same suggestions for evaluating the effectiveness of activities and exercises.

1.   Students' reading habits can be evaluated by use of student surveys or interviews, by packaged assessment programs like Accelerated Reader, or by some in-house record keeping system. Several good standardized tests exist for testing reading progression.

2.   Visual literacy can be evaluated by observing students' own visual designs—from drawings, graphic designs, and photographs to motion pictures and computer graphics. Students must also be able to verbally analyze various images they perceive and to interpret the messages delivered.

3.   Listening skills are evaluated by observing the students' ability to follow oral directions, to remember facts and details, and to retell a series of pieces of information. Standardized or teacher-made tests can pre-test and post-test listening skills mastery.

4.   Media literacy is evaluated by observing students' use of equipment needed to create productions and noting the final product of media projects for appropriateness of format, length and depth of coverage, graphic quality, and focus.

Skill 4.5   Identify methods for motivating and assisting students to use, analyze, and evaluate various media

Motivational techniques are derived from child development needs. Obviously, students must receive personal satisfaction from any pursuit, but some students for whom the reward of pleasure is not enough must have other stimulants.

Some motivational techniques:

1.   The classroom teacher's approval of using different media as an integral part of learning. Students will emulate the opinions and practices of persons they respect. Involve the teachers, and the students will follow. However, the media used should be current and appropriate to the learning needs.

2. The availability of current equipment which is in good condition. Many students have computers and video equipment in their own homes. Sometimes the quality of their equipment and their skill in using it exceeds that of the school's equipment and expertise. Students want to experiment with emerging technologies and create quality productions.

3. Students will also be encouraged to participate in projects if they see the external rewards of a particular activity. These activities may include producing media for graded class projects or contests, being asked to preview media for its appropriateness for classroom use ,or helping to develop products that will be seen by parent or community groups.

Skill 4.6   Identify methods for encouraging students to establish the habit of using resources and information agencies for lifelong learning

Students need to know the variety of information resources and agencies available to them and be given frequent opportunities to use them in order to establish good habits. By learning about the resources available outside the school, they will more likely pursue using these services in adulthood.

1. Inform them of resource sharing networks—public and academic libraries, Internet services, and community agencies—that provide information. Some schools in districts with fully automated public library systems may provide online access to the public library catalog from a terminal at the school site. Public libraries also offer on-line cataloging services that can be accessed from home computers and some are now providing access to the Internet. Community colleges and universities encourage high school students to share their facilities for information gathering.

2. Invite representatives from other information agencies to promote their programs through the schools. Post public library hours, advertisements of lectures, book reviews, or other library activities; arrange for guest speakers from Internet providers or radio and television stations; and participate in field trips to other information centers

COMPETENCY 5.0   KNOWLEDGE OF METHODS OF ASSISTING FACULTY AND STUDENTS IN DESIGNING AND PRODUCING RESOURCES

Skill 5.1   Determine when it is appropriate to design and produce resources

In the last twenty years, audio-visual materials and computer-based resources, once considered supplementary to instruction, have become instructional media, integral parts of the instructional process. Students and teachers should learn not only to use commercial products but to design and produce their own materials. It is appropriate for faculty to produce their own resources when:

1.   Commercial products are unavailable, unsuited to learning styles/preferences/environments, or too costly.
2.   Teaching styles indicate a preference for non-commercial products.
3.   Teachers have the expertise and necessary equipment for original production.

It is appropriate for students to produce their own resources when:

1.   Achieving understanding with non-verbal means of expression.
2.   Communicating ideas and information to others.
3.   Expressing creativity.
4.   Demonstrating mastery of lesson objectives by alternative means.

Skill 5.2   Determine what resources should be produced to meet a specific instructional need

Having determined that it is appropriate to use teacher or student produced media, it is necessary to determine which media should be produced to meet the specific instructional need. School library media specialists may produce media for two purposes:

1.   To make presentations for information skills instruction, other teacher-directed activities, or testing.
2.   To make materials to be placed directly in the hands of students.

Many excellent books on media instruction detail the instructional uses of media formats. These uses are largely contingent on the goals of a given lesson or activity. Here are two goals for a lesson along with the suggestions for media that will accomplish with these goals.

1. **Introduction.** Several formats allow large group listening or viewing and are appropriate for introducing new materials. These formats include filmstrips, films, slidetapes, computer projection, overhead transparencies and videotapes. These formats can require a large screen, an elevated monitor or multiple units for viewing. With young learners who are non-readers, display boards with large print and audiocassettes for story-telling are most effective.

2. **Application.** During this phase, media that lend themselves to individual or small group use are needed. As students investigate the subject matter, organize that information, practice, or demonstrate understanding, they may create any or several types of media. With young children these would include manipulatives (e.g., building blocks, letters, numbers or shapes formed with cloth, plastic or wood). Older students would create photographs/slides, audiocassette tapes or videotapes. Some secondary students might even design their own computer programs. Students at all levels can be taught to use computer design software to create multi-media productions.

The introduction and application of media production techniques helps the user, whether child or adult, clarify his or her own objectives and determine the exact format which would best present the ideas and achieve selected goals. A lesson on distinguishing the calls of local birds might introduce the material using audiocassette tapes while recognizing plumage would use slides or videotape. Students preparing a study of estuarine ecology might incorporate video and computer graphics designed from electron microscope imagery to demonstrate their applied knowledge of the various micro-organisms in the local river.

Skill 5.3   Identify techniques for planning, designing, and evaluating media

Once the determination to produce media has been made, there is a process for planning, designing, and evaluating the product.

Planning:

1. State the main idea (goal) of the production, clearly and concisely.
2. Determine the purpose of the product.
    a. To provide information or develop appreciation. Media with this purpose is general in nature, usually meant for presentation to a class or larger group acting as passive listeners. However, it must use dramatic or motivational appeals to hold audience interest.
    b. To provide instruction. Designed for individual or small group use, instructive media should be specific, systematic and interactive.
3. Develop the objectives. State specifically what the audience should know or be able to do after using this media and what measurements will be used to determine their knowledge or ability.
4. Analyze the audience. Determine ability and interest, learning styles, and current understanding of the topic.
5. Research the idea. Use print, non-print and human resources to study both the subject matter and the media techniques/formats to best present the subject matter.

Once a plan is created, the next stage is to design the material:

1. Prepare an outline of the content. Create story board cards for each subheading and match them to the objectives.
2. Select the media format(s) to communicate the idea. Consider time, effort and cost as well as audio-visual needs. If motion and sound are not essential, consider using transparencies or slides since they are easier to make and require no editing. Consider the equipment and facilities available.
3. Create the content. Prepare a story board delineating the description of each graphic and write a corresponding script if captions or sound narration will be included.
4. Create the media.

Once the materials are designed, the media specialist will want to evaluate the effectiveness of the materials as they are presented to the group. Evaluation is the final stage for creating and implementing instructional media. Here are some tips for evaluating materials:

1. Observe reaction of audience to resources. Body language and verbal reactions, especially in younger children, will indicate the level of interest.
2. Solicit verbal or written reactions to appearance, arrangement, and technical quality as well as ease of understanding and mastery of content.
3. Examine costs. Determine if costs of materials and time invested were equal to outcomes.

Skill 5.4   Identify basic methods of producing graphic, video, audio, computer, and photographic presentations and resources

Specific methods of producing graphic, photographic, audio, video and computer media are dealt with extensively in the resources cited. However, production of media formats generally involve the need to

1. Determine display format—easel or wall board, poster, hand-out, transparency, video, or computer generated.
2. Plan art work—lettering font, size, margin, mount, visual layout, color/shading, and lighting.
3. Select materials—paper, laminating film, or photographic film.
4. Select production equipment—calligraphy pens, copy stand, camera, computer, video camera, and audio equipment.
5. Complete the process following plan/storyboard. Letter, draw, photograph, shoot film, and merge graphics/text.
6. Organize and edit. Put display in order, dub audio track to edited videotape. Plan time for recreating any art work with technical flaws.
7. Package the product. Burn to CD/ DVD, laminate posters, photocopy hand-outs, and add credits.

COMPETENCY 6.0 KNOWLEDGE OF METHODS FOR DESIGN AND DELIVERY OF STAFF DEVELOPMENT

Skill 6.1 Identify methods for teaching staff how to use equipment and how to select, use, evaluate, and produce media

Staff, including teachers and support personnel, should be offered periodic in-service in learning new skills and reinforcing known skills. These skills may be taught at formal, structured workshops or in informal small-group or individual sessions when a need arises.

1. A hands-on orientation for teachers new to school to familiarize them with available resource and equipment and apprise them of services. The orientation should include information on incorporating appropriate media into their lessons. Written procedures for selection and evaluation should be available. The specialist should use a variety of media formats in presenting the information, such as overhead transparencies or LED projections for lists and forms; a video program on producing videos, slideshows and audio; and the automated card catalog for search procedures.

2. Provide information on new and existing media and solicit recommendations.
    a. Frequently send bibliographies, catalogs or newsletters, asking for purchase suggestions.
    b. Inform all teachers of district and school preview policies and arrange previews for purchase suggestions.
    c. Involve as many teachers as possible on review committees.

3. Periodically provide brief refresher modules. Advertise the media and equipment to be used in each session. Suggest uses of potential lessons for each media format so teachers can make appropriate choices. Have teachers create one or more products at each session that can be used for instruction in an upcoming lesson.

4. Secure oral or written feedback on both teacher-made and commercial media used in classroom lessons. Ask teachers to use appropriate evaluation criteria in measuring the product's worth. The more familiar they become with the criteria, the better their product choices will become.

Skill 6.2   Identify the elements of effective staff development.

The design of a staff development activity is similar to a basic lesson profile with accommodations and special considerations for adult learners. The following steps should used when planning and implementing training for members of the school learning community.

1. Analyze learner styles. Adult learners are more receptive to role playing and individual performance before a group. Learner motivation is more internal, but some external motivations, such as release time, compensatory time, in service credit or some written recognition, might be discussed with the principal.
2. Assess learner needs. Conduct a survey among teachers to determine which media or equipment they want to learn more about. Consider environmental factors such as time, place and temperature. Since many in service activities occur after school, taking the lesson to the teachers in their own classrooms may make them more comfortable especially if they can have a reviving afternoon snack. If they must come to the media center, serve refreshments.
3. Select performance objectives. Determine exactly what the teacher should be able to do at the end of a successful in service session.
4. Plan activities to achieve objectives. Demonstrate the skill to be taught, involve the participants in active performance and production, and allow for practice and feedback.
5. Select appropriate resources. Arrange that all materials and equipment are ready and in good functioning order on the day of the in service.
6. Determine instructor. Either the school library media specialist or a faculty member should conduct these on-site in services unless the complexity or novelty of the technology requires an outside expert.
7. Provide continuing support. This support is the key to making staff development effective. Staff are most likely to continue to use what they've learned when they know they will be able to receive assistance with implementation. The instructor or designated substitute should be available after the in service for reinforcement.
8. Evaluation. Determine the effectiveness of the in service and make modifications as recommended in future in services

Skill 6.3   Identify methods to assist staff in the application of new and emerging technologies to meet varied learning needs

Because we are in the business of teaching, all technologies must be viewed as educational tools. To enable teachers to understand the way these technologies can be applied in their classrooms, they must understand the relationship between these tools and learning needs. The school library media professionals must be able to update teachers on this correlation.

1.   Conduct timely, short in-service activities to demonstrate and allow teachers to manipulate new technologies and plan classroom uses.

2.   Clip articles or write reviews to distribute to teachers with suggestions for application in their particular learning environment.

3.   Offer to plan and teach lessons in different content areas.

COMPETENCY 7.0   KNOWLEDGE OF METHODS AND RESOURCES FOR PROVIDING INFORMATION

Skill 7.1   Identify methods for selecting resources that meet the information needs of students and staff

One of the fallacies of education is that all good teachers keep abreast of changes in education by reading professional journals. Many do and most try, but the volume of available material is overwhelming.

Since the school library media center houses general professional materials and knowledge of the contents of these materials is one of the specialist's responsibilities, a vehicle for communicating information to teachers is important. A two-part NCR form that identifies the receiver, the resource title and date of publication, and a concise summary of the contents is easiest. Sometimes a photocopy of relevant portions of the article can be attached to the form. Save one part of each form for your own program evaluation.

Education Digest, Phi Delta Kappan, and *Educational Leadership* are outstanding trend evaluators. Such magazines as *Teacher* give information about grants and services for both students and educators alike. Each year FAME sponsors the Jim Harbin Student Media Festival. Students in four age groupings devise up to ten-minute programs in a variety of media. Winners' productions are presented at the annual FAME conference. This is an excellent project for television production classes, but it is also a way to involve content classes in learning through media production. Look to the annual fall edition of the *Florida Media Quarterly* for complete details and application forms.

Of course, changes in school board policies, legislative actions, and DOE publications are usually channeled through the media specialists. The Florida DOE *Monday Report* is accessible through FIRN (the Florida Information Resources Network) and printed copies are sent to all school principals. Your principal may be delighted to have you offer to communicate information from that and other reports to teachers.

Skill 7.2   Identify the characteristics of an effective system for organizing information resources to meet the needs of students and staff

Resource organization systems vary from school to school, based on factors such as user demand, storage considerations, staff limitations and preferences, and processing procedures. Some media specialists separate specific age/reading level collections for ease of location, especially with younger children. Audio-visual and multi-media kits may be shelved with print material if they can be circulated to all users. Visibility creates greater use. However, collection security for instructional materials and equipment must also be considered. Organizational procedures should be logical and follow standardized procedures as much as possible.

Here are the objectives of organization systems:

1.   Ready access. To make resources easy to locate, regardless of format, a bibliographic control system must be in place. A catalog, preferably automated, should include all print and non-print resources and equipment. *Florida School Media Programs: A Guide for Excellence* recommends that all school-owned media should appear in the media center catalog regardless of where they are housed.

2.   Circulation ease. If the card catalog is not automated, the media center staff should keep accurate circulation records to facilitate retrieval and inventory. If audio-visual materials or equipment are not housed near the circulation area, a paper record is necessary. For equipment not housed in the media center itself, location information must appear in the catalog.

Skill 7.3   Identify factors that influence access to information

Providing access to information is one of the most crucial roles of the school library media specialist. Kinds of access include intellectual, physical, flexibility, and climate characteristics.

In providing intellectual access to information, school library media centers should be places that promote a full range of information formats and services that meet the needs of the staff and students.

Aisles wide enough for wheelchairs, shelf height appropriate for the age of student, and a user friendly room arrangement are just a few ways to provide physical access to information in the school library media center. For students who are physically challenged, it is important to have devices that increase the usability of resources. This can include various formats of information such as audiobooks or books in Braille format.

Flexible access to resources is conducive to encouraging just–in–time learning. Resources should be available at the point of need, and collaboration with classroom teachers makes flexible access even more effective.

The final factor is the climate of the school library media center. It should be a warm and inviting place where staff and students feel free to come and learn and use the resources available. The school library media specialist plays an essential role in creating and maintaining a welcoming climate.

Skill 7.4 Identify relevant information agencies and resources outside the school.

In this day of online resources, access to information can feel both overwhelming and limitless. There are innumerable agencies and resources for almost any information need. The ability to ferret out and identify these agencies and resources is part of the skill set of the competent library media specialist.

Ideas for places to start when locating relevant information agencies and resources include:

- **Public libraries**—many libraries now have reference librarians on-call (via phone or e-mail) 24/7 to direct you to appropriate resources. It's important to encourage students and faculty to use not just the school media library but to avail themselves of the services of *all* libraries.
- **Federal Agencies Directory**—http://www.lib.lsu.edu/gov/fedgov.html
- **Reference volumes**—dictionaries, thesauruses, almanacs, maps, encyclopedias, and the like.
- **Publications from governing bodies**—ALA or ASLA book and media reviews

Every community and every school will offer varying degrees of access to information. The role of the media specialist is to facilitate the highest level of access using all resources available.

Skill 7.5   Identify considerations necessary for participation in resource sharing

Resource sharing has always been an integral part of education. Before the technology revolution, the sharing was done within schools or departments and between teachers. Now it is possible to access information around the world.

Resource sharing is a way of

1.   Providing a broader information base to enable users to find and access the resources that provide the needed information.
2.   Reducing or containing media center budgets.
3.   Establishing cooperation with other resource providers that encourage mutual planning and standardization of control.

Resource sharing systems include:

1.   **Interlibrary loan**. The advent of computer databases has simplified the process of locating sources in other libraries. Local public library collections can be accessed from terminals in the media center. Physical access depends on going to the branch where the material is housed.
2.   **Networking systems**. Sharing information has become even easier with the use of network services. Files can be shared and accessed from room to room, school to school and city to city. Resources can be shared within a small geographic location such as a school by the use of a local area network, or LAN. A wide area network, or WAN, is used to communicate over a larger area such as a school district or city.
    a.   E-mail allows educators to communicate across the state.
    b.   On-line services (i.e., Internet providers) offer access to a specific menu of locations. Monthly fees and time charges must be budgeted.
    c.   Individual city or county network systems. These are community sponsored networks, often part of the public library system, which provide Internet access for the price of a local phone call. A time limit usually confines an individual search to allow more users access.
    d.   On-line continuing education programs offer courses and degrees through at-home study. Large school districts provide lessons for homebound students or home school advocates.
    e.   Bulletin boards allow individuals or groups to converse electronically with persons in another place.

Telecommunications. Using telephone and television as the media for communication, telecommunications is used primarily for distance learning. Many universities or networks of universities provide workshops, conferences and college credit courses for educators. They also offer courses for senior high school students in subjects that could not generate adequate class counts in their home schools. Large school districts offer broadcast programming for homebound or home schooled students. The advantage of telecommunication programming (as opposed to networking systems) is that students are provided with a phone number so they can interact with the instructors or information providers.

Skill 7.6   Identify techniques to provide specific information in response to reference requests

There are three types of reference requests depending on the depth of the question and the scope of the search. However, some very simple questions can lead to complex searches.

1.   Ready reference request. These requests usually require a limited search in standard reference books (encyclopedias, atlases, almanacs) or electronic databases (SIRS Researcher, Grolier's Encyclopedia, 3D Atlas, or American Heritage Dictionary and Thesaurus). The request is satisfied by directing the requestor to the exact sources in which the information may be found. Occasionally, a seemingly simple question cannot be answered quickly and thus necessitates a higher level search.

A request for the names of the current governor and cabinet can be found easily in *The Florida Handbook* or *Taylor's Encyclopedia of Government Officials*. However, a request for biographical information about an obscure or subject- specific person may require delving into many biographical dictionaries or encyclopedias.

If the library carries the *Who's Who in America* and *Who Was Who in America* series, an American is easy to identify. However, most school library media centers do not purchase biographical dictionaries of foreign persons unless they were noteworthy in a particular profession. *Who's Who in Science, Current Biography, Webster's Biographical Dictionary, British Writers Before 1900* are some helpful resources.

2.   Specific need requests. These requests are the most frequently addressed and may range from merely steering the requestor to a card catalog, index or other bibliographic aid if the user is familiar with those tools. Specific needs requests are especially useful if students are working on a lengthy project and resources must be found outside the school, and the user may need instruction in using search tools and locating the resources.

A student debater may want to know which resources would give statistics about teen pregnancy. A teacher may ask which books and periodicals have the best articles on inclusion of special education students.

The answer to specific need questions entails locating the resources by identifying the proper search tools (e.g., card catalog, the *Reader's Guide to Periodical Literature*, or automated indexes like *Infotrac* or *Newsbank*).

3. Research request. This question is encountered most often in secondary school, university and academic libraries. The search is broader in scope and requires more time. Any specific need request could be expanded into a research request.

A debater may be preparing a portfolio for a contest and needs photocopies of available material. A teacher taking a college course may ask the school library media specialist to pull periodical articles relating to inclusion. These requests may require using on-line databases and research queries outside the library media center.

Research services are gaining wider need as users are confronted with great amounts of information as they have less time to conduct their searches.

Skill 7.7   Identify the most appropriate resources for responding to a specific information need

Selecting appropriate materials requires knowledge of the resource tools.

1. Companies who offer collection lists designed for elementary, middle, or secondary schools or for special content schools—vocational or performing arts. These lists are used most often for opening a new school library media center. School library media specialists and review committees customize these lists to user needs.

2. Publisher's catalogs. These are good starting points for locating specific titles and comparison shopping.

3. Vendors representing one or more publishers. Too little has been said about establishing good relationships with vendors who have access to demonstration materials and can make them available for review. Naturally, they want to sell their employers' products; however, most are familiar with their competitors' product lines and work collaboratively to help schools secure the most appropriate materials.

4. Review publications. *School Library Journal* and *Booklist* offer concise reviews on current books. *Children and Books* [resource #45] contains a thorough list of book selection aids. *Technology Review, New Media,* and other media and technology magazines offer evaluation of audio-visual and computer software and hardware.

5. Bibliographic indexes of subject specific titles with summaries. These indexes are not free and are most cost effective if housed in the district professional library. The same is true of *Books in Print*, in print and non-print formats. Because its contents change significantly from year to year, many districts cannot justify its cost, relying instead on direct communication with publishers to determine a book's status.

Methods:

1. Review resources using existing tools. The school library media center staff should gather information concerning contents and cost of considered items and budget allocation figures.

2. Organize a review committee. This may be a district committee for selection of materials to be purchased for several schools or a local committee (the library media advisory committee if one exists) for selection of specific titles or series. The committee should be composed mainly of teachers, representing a cross-section of grade levels and subject areas.

   At the district review, involving large numbers of items, the district supervisor may have items available for on-site preview. If possible, the school committee should have products available for examination. Ask a vendor to make a presentation.

3. Use the material in a classroom setting for an immediate evaluation of its worth. Naturally, this method requires that a faculty member--teacher or library media specialist--preview the item first to determine its suitability for the intended audience.

   Preferably, written records of all reviews should be kept in the district media office. Most districts have a preview form for rating an item against evaluative criteria.

COMPETENCY 8.0 KNOWLEDGE OF RESOURCES IN ALL FORMATS FOR CHILDREN AND ADOLESCENTS

Skill 8.1 Identify materials that are recognized as outstanding in their medium

In addition to the works of Carlsen, Donelson, Huck, and Sutherland, all of which contain excellent information on children's/adolescent interests and needs, the school library media specialist can rely on lists of titles published in other resources. The *School Library Media Annual* includes Caldecott and Newbery winners and notable materials lists such as

1. Notable Books for Children - Association for Library Service to Children of ALA.

2. Children's Reviewers' Choice - Booklist.

3. Children's Choices - The Children's Book Council.

4. Best Books for Young Adults - Young Adult Services Division of ALA.

5. Young Adult Reviewer's Choice - Booklist.

6. Notable Children's Films - ALSC.

7. Selected Films for Young Adults - YASD.

In Florida a committee of FAME annually selects the Sunshine State Young Reader's Award recipients, printing the winners in the spring or summer issue of *Florida Media Quarterly*. Winners include:

Grades 3-5

2003-04	*Touching Spirit Bear* Ben Mikaelsen
2000	*Me Tarzan* Byars Betsy
2000-01	*Because of Winn Dixie* Kate Dicamillio
	The Ghost in Room 11 Betty Ren Wright
1995-96	*Blackwater Swamp* Bill Wallace
1994-95	*Knights of the Kitchen Table* Jon Scieszka
1993-94	*Fudge-A-Mania* Judy Blume
1992-93	*Fudge* Charlotte Towner Graeber
	No Bean Sprouts Please Constance Hiser
	The Doll in the Garden Mary Downing Hahn

Grades 6-8

2000-01	*The Ghost of Fossil Glen* Cynthia Defelice
2001-02	*Among the Hidden* Margaret Haddix
1995-96	*Seventh-Grade Weirdo* Lee Wardlow
1994-95	*Devil's Bridge* Cynthia DeFelice
1993-94	*Nightmare* Willo Davis Roberts
1992-93	*Something Upstairs* Avi
	A Doll in the Garden Mary Downing Hahn
	The Devil's Arithmetic Jane Yolen

Lists of Caldecott and Newbery awards can also be found in most general encyclopedias.

Though bookseller John Newbery was the first to publish literature for children on any scale in the second half of 18th century England, the great outpouring of children's literature came 100 years later in the Victorian Age. Novels such as Charles Dickens' *Oliver Twist*, Robert Louis Stevenson's *Treasure Island*, and Rudyard Kipling's *Jungle Book*, have become classics in children's literature, even though they were not solely written for children. These books not only helped children understand the world they lived in, but the books also satisfied their interest in adventure.

Many of the most popular books for children in the late 19th and early 20th century were translations of foreign favorites like Andrew Lang's *The Blue Fairy Book* (and its rainbow of successors); Astrid Lingren's *Pippa Longstocking*; Johanna Spyri's *Heidi*; and Jean de Burnhoff's Babar Series. Titles in English such as Beatrix Potter's *Tales*; A.A. Milne's *Winnie the Pooh;* and Kenneth Grahame's *Wind in the Willows* have remained popular into the 1990's. The beauty of many of these books is their universality of appeal.

Children's/adolescent literature of the last 50 years has grown to thousands of new titles per year and many tend to the trendy, the authors and publishers being very aware of the market and the social changes affecting their products. Books are selected for libraries because of their social, psychological, and intellectual value. Collections must also contain materials that recognize cultural and ethnic needs. Because so many popular titles, especially in the young adult area, deal with controversial subjects, school library media specialists are faced with juggling the preferences of their student patrons with the need to provide worthwhile literature and maintain intellectual freedom in the face of increasing censorship. Books such as Robert Cormier's *Chocolate War, Return to Chocolate War,* and *Fade* deal with the darker side of teen life. Paul Zindel's *Pigman* and *The Undertaker's Gone Bananas* deal with the stresses in teen life with a touch of humor.

Books of the young child reader teach about his relationships to the world around him and to other people and things in that world. They help him learn how things operate and how to overcome his fears. Like the still popular fairy tales of previous centuries, some of today's popular children's books are fantasies or allegories, such as Robert O'Brien's *Mrs. Frisby and the Rats of NIMH*.

Popular books for preadolescents deal more with establishing relationships with members of the opposite sex (e.g., Sweet Valley High series) and learning to cope with their changing bodies, personalities or life situations, as displayed in Judy Blume's *Are You There, God? It's Me, Margaret*. Adolescents are still interested in the fantasy and science fiction genres as well as the popular juvenile fiction. Middle school students still read the *Little House on the Prairie* series and the mysteries of the Hardy Boys and Nancy Drew. Teens value the works of Emily and Charlotte Brontë, Willa Cather, Jack London, William Shakespeare and Mark Twain as much as those of Piers Anthony, S.E. Hinton, Madeleine L'Engle, Stephen King and J.R.R. Tolkien. Despite their publication dates, most children are still enthralled in the classics of English literature.

Skill 8.2   Identify authors who are recognized as outstanding in their genre

Well-known writers of children's fiction include Betty Byars, Susan Cooper, Shirley Hughes, Sheila Solomon Klass, Elizabeth Speare, Gary K. Wolf and Lawrence Yep. Children's poets include Nancy Larrick, Maurice Sendak and Shel Silverstein.

Fiction writers popular with young adolescents include Judy Blume, Alice Childress, Beverly Cleary, Roald Dahl, Virginia Hamilton, Kathryn Lasky, Lois Lowry, Robin McKinley, Katherine Paterson, Teresa Tomlinson and Bill Wallace.

Older adolescents also enjoy the writers in these genres:

1.   Fantasy: Piers Anthony, Ursula LeGuin and Ann McCaffrey
2.   Horror: V.C. Andrews and Stephen King
3.   Juvenile fiction: Judy Blume, Robert Cormier, Rosa Guy, Virginia Hamilton, S.E. Hinton, M.E. Kerr, Harry Mazer, Norma Fox Mazer, Richard Newton Peck, Cynthia Voight and Paul Zindel
4.   Science fiction: Isaac Asimov, Ray Bradbury, Arthur C.Clarke, Frank Herbert, Larry Niven and H.G. Wells

Skill 8.3   Identify illustrators who are recognized as outstanding in their medium

Each year an outstanding illustrator of a children's book is honored for his or her outstanding work by being presented with the Caldecott Medal. This award was created in honor of Randolph Caldecott and is distributed annually by the *Association for Library Service for Children.* It was first presented in 1938.

Award winners for the past fifteen years include:
  2007 - *Flotsam* by David Wiesner
  2006 - *The Hello, Goodbye Window* illustrated by Chris Raschka and written by Norton Juster
  2005 - *Kitten's First Full Moon* by Kevin Henkes
  2004 - *The Man Who Walked Between the Towers* by Mordicai Gerstein
  2003 - *My Friend Rabbit* by Eric Rohmann
  2002 - *The Three Pigs* by David Wiesner
  2001 - *So You Want to Be President?* illustrated by David Small and written by Judith St. George
  2000 - *Had a Little Overcoat* by Simms Taback
  1999 - Snowflake Bentley illustrated by Mary Azarian and written by Jacqueline Briggs Martin
  1998 - *Rapunzel* by Paul O. Zelinsky
  1997 - *Golem* by David Wisniewski
  1996 - *Officer Buckle and Gloria* by Peggy Rathmann
  1995 - *Smoky Night* illustrated by David Diaz; text: Eve Bunting
  1994 - *Grandfather's Journey* by Allen Say and edited by Walter Lorraine
  1993 - *Mirette on the High Wire* by Emily Arnold McCully

Notable illustrators of children's books include Marcia Brown, Leo and Diane Dillon, Barbara Dooney, Nonny Hogrogian, David Macaulay, Emily Arnold McCully, Allen Say, Maurice Sendak, Chris Van Allsburg and David Wiesner.

Skill 8.4   Identify resources recognized as outstanding in meeting the psychological, social, and intellectual needs of youth

See Skill 8.2

Skill 8.5   Identify the major electronic services and bibliographic databases through which resources for children and adolescents can be located

See Skill 7.7.

Skill 8.6   Identify the major on-line resources available through each of the electronic services and bibliographic databases

There are a wide variety of internet resources available to assist school library media specialists with providing access to current information. Below are several information resources. More online resources can be found in 3.5.

Periodical Directories

Ulrich's International Periodicals Directory
- offers complete and current reference for select periodicals and serials
- collects information from over 80,000 worldwide serials publishers
- contains annuals, continuations, conference proceedings

SIRS Enduring Issues
- print versions contains eight volumes and 32-topics
- highlights the best articles published during the preceding year

Public Affairs Information Service (PAIS)
- references over 553,300 journal articles, books, documents directories and reports

Indexes

The New York Times
- assists with locating articles and information printed in the New York Times newspaper
- Searchable by topic and uses the words "see also" to suggest other subject headings

Professional Journals

The Library Quarterly
- scholarly research regarding all areas of librarianship

School Library Media Research
- is published by American Association of School Librarians
- is the successor to *School Library Media Quarterly Online*
- Its purpose is to provide research concerning the management, implementation, and evaluation of school library media programs

Library Trends
- explores critical trends in professional librarianship
- includes practical applications and literature reviews

Library Power
- is a research study that proved the viability of school libraries as a vehicle to promote student achievement

American Libraries
- is published by the American Library Association
- provides the latest news and updates from the association

School Library Journal
- serves school and public librarians who work with the young
- provides information needed to integrate libraries into all aspects of the school curriculum
- provides resources to become effective technology leaders
- provides resources to assist with collection development

YA (Voice of Youth Advocates)
- focuses on librarians and educators working with young adults
- founded by Dorothy M. Broderick and Mary K. Chelton

School Library Media Activities Monthly Magazine
- designed for K-8 school library media specialists
- focuses on collaboratively planned units with teachers
- stresses importance of introducing reference materials

Knowledge Quest
- published by The American Association of School Librarians
- designed to assist with the development of school library media programs

COMPETENCY 9.0 KNOWLEDGE OF THE DESIGN, PLANNING, AND DEVELOPMENT OF A LIBRARY MEDIA PROGRAM

Skill 9.1 Identify school and student characteristics that influence the mission of the library media program

The mission of any organization, business or educational institution should evolve from the needs and expectations of its customers. In the case of the school library media center, its mission must parallel the school's mission and attend to the users' needs for resources and services.

The school library media program should examine school and student characteristics.

School:

1.   The mission of the school library media center should reflect and be in harmony with the stated school mission.
2.   The program's mission should reflect the curricular direction of the school, whether the school is academic, vocational, compensatory.
3.   The mission should reflect the willingness of the administration and faculty to support the program.

Student:

1.   The mission is influenced by pupil demographics that include age, achievement and ability levels, reading levels, and learning styles.
2.   The mission may indicate the students' interest in self- directed learning and exploratory reading.
3.   The mission reflects support from parents and community groups.

Once a mission has been defined, it is important to assess the current status of the program and see how closely it follows that mission. Gathering this information is essential to the formation of effective goals and objectives.

Skill 9.2   Distinguish between a library media program goal and an objective.

A goal is a broad statement of an intended outcome, which gives direction to the program and projects a long-range priority.

An objective is a specific statement of a measurable result that will occur by a particular time (i.e., it must specify the conditions and criteria to be met effectively).

Using an Olympic athlete as an example, an appropriate set of goals and objectives might go as follows:

Goal: To win an Olympic Medal.
Objectives:

1.   To increase my speed by .05 seconds per meter by June 30.
2.   To double my practice time during the two weeks before the competition begins.
3.   To lose 3 lbs. before my weigh-in.

If translated into goals and objectives for library media centers, the set may read as the following:

Goal: To develop a collection more suited to the academic demands of the curriculum

Objectives:

1.   To increase non-fiction collection by 10% in the next school year.
2.   To ensure readability levels suited to gifted students for 5% of new selections.

Goal: To provide telecommunications services within three years.

Objectives:

1.   To design a model for instructional use in 1996.
2.   To plan for equipment and facilities needs in 1997.
3.   To implement the model with a control group in 1998.

Skill 9.3   Determine characteristics of a long-range plan for a library media program

A goal is a long-range plan. An objective is a short-range plan. Therefore, when planning a school library media program based on an assessment of school and student characteristics, the program planning team should factor in these elements.

A long-range plan should

1.   Extend from 3-5 years.
2.   Incorporate the goals of the other departments (grade levels or content teams) in the school.
3.   Be stated in terms that are non-limiting. The goal should be an achievable aim, not a pipe dream.

Long-range plans may evolve from district plans for school-to-school connectivity and resource sharing plans as well as from goals that match the local school goals. Preferably, these goals would be included in the School Improvement Plan, and often it is the library media specialist who chairs the technology committee. The 3-5 year plan should address the learning objectives and the technology needed to meet those objectives. It should also project the cost of hardware, software, phone time charges, and peripherals. Finally, the long-range plans should prioritize the goals and objectives.

Skill 9.4   Determine characteristics of a short-range plan for a library media program

A short-range plan should be one part of a longer range plan that is

1.   Accomplishable in one year or less.
2.   Linked meaningfully in a logical progression to the expressed goal.
3.   Flexible, as most objectives must be processed through affected groups before finalization.

The short-range plan should address one or more priorities and the following related factors:

1.   Immediate cost and funding sources.
2.   Implementation. What type of hardware, software and peripherals should be purchased to meet the goals? Are there networking considerations (e.g., cabling, electrical outlets, surge protection)? Are there concerns about the use of certain technologies (e.g., multi-user contracts, dedicated phone lines, monitoring systems for student access to Internet sites)?

3.   Flexibility. Does the technology have durability and potential future use? Is it upgradable or does it have possible use elsewhere if new or upgraded technology becomes available? Can the goals be adjusted easily as needs change?

Skill 9.5   Identify the typical purposes of the school library media advisory committee

There are several justifications for a school library media advisory committee. First, all groups affected by the library media program are given an opportunity to provide input during the planning, implementation, and evaluation process.

Second, a cooperative plan ensures that all participants accept and promote the program. Third, though slower in completion, a committee-directed plan alleviates having the media specialist shoulder decision-making alone.

No specific guidelines exist for the organization of a library media advisory committee. However, representation from administration, faculty, student body, and parents is essential. The number of participants is affected by student body size and the extent of parent involvement. In elementary schools with active PTA's there may be as many parents as teachers. In secondary schools where parents take a less active role in their children's education, the committee may struggle to find one parent. Students may be nominated by the faculty, may volunteer, or may be members of a student government subcommittee. Each grade level or content area should have teacher representation, and the principal or her administrative designee should serve.

The role of leader usually falls to the media specialist, though an elected adult chairperson who is not a media specialist is preferable. It is too easy in some schools for the media specialist to do all the work, while the committee merely rubber stamps his or her decisions and actions.

Some of the activities performed by a library media advisory committee fall into the following four areas.

1.   Collection development.
      - making decisions about the purchase of audio-visual equipment and
        technology hardware and software.
      - assisting with collection weeding.
      - reviewing challenged material.
2.   Program planning.
      - reviewing policies and procedures.
      - setting priorities.
      - allocating the budget.

3.   Operation (volunteering).
       - teaching information skills.
       - raising funds, especially through book fairs.
       - producing promotional materials (bulletin boards, newsletters, manuals).
4.   Evaluation
       - preparing and tabulating results of needs assessment surveys.

Conveniently scheduled meetings should be held regularly, with a specific agenda and minutes. Problem solving activities with specific, attainable goals should be followed by implementation of the solution. Reports of meetings should be communicated to students, teachers and parent groups.

Skill 9.6   Identify ways the library media program can support school improvement.

There are many ways in which the school library media specialists can support school improvement. Possibilities include:

- Collaborate with teachers to plan integrated learning activities.
- Educate students and staff in the processes of information literacy.
- Work closely with school and district-level planning teams.
- Develop a thorough working knowledge of the grade level curriculum.
- Assemble a collection of resources that meet the needs of students and the curriculum.
- Work closely with district, state, and national committees to develop curriculum.
- Work closely with parents, community members and outside agencies to enhance educational activities.

COMPETENCY 10.0   KNOWLEDGE OF PROCEDURES TO EVALUATE THE EFFECTIVENESS OF A SCHOOL LIBRARY MEDIA PROGRAM

Skill 10.1   Identify components, participants and strategies for a comprehensive evaluation of the library media program

Evaluation requires standards, the conditions that should exist if the program is to be judged successful. Some of these standards may already be determined by national or state guidelines that district administrators have agreed to maintain. Sometimes, a district operates without a program to guide school library media centers. In that case each school must be responsible not only for setting its own criteria but also for inspiring some district planning.

If a school seeks or wishes to maintain accreditation with the Southern Association of Colleges and Schools (SAC), using that organization's recommendations is an excellent way to set program goals and objectives. Because SAC requires every accredited school to conduct an intensive ten year reevaluation and five year interim reviews, the library media center program planners may wish to coordinate their own study with the SAC's reviews. *Florida Information Skills K-12* offers qualitative standards for the teaching of skills that can be used in the evaluation process.

A wide variety of evaluation criteria may be used. The criteria may be:

1.   Diagnostic. These are standards based on conditions existing in programs that have already been judged as excellent.
2.   Projective. These standards are guidelines for conditions as they ought to be.
3.   Quantitative. These standards require numerical measurement.
4.   Qualitative. These standards are designed to express essentially the measured criteria as quantitative without exact numerical amounts. Action research is a form of qualitative data collection that occurs when educators reflect upon their teaching by observing occurrences in a school or classroom and identifying problems. The educator then devises steps or actions to correct the problem.

Skill 10.2   Determine strategies for analyzing the results of library media program evaluations

Most school library media program evaluations have been diagnostic or qualitative. Diagnostic prescriptions alone make no allowances for specific conditions in given schools and are often interpreted too liberally; in addition, qualitative prescriptions alone are difficult to measure or sustain. Projective standards are usually broad national guidelines which are best used as long-range goals. Preferably, a program evaluation utilizing a combination of quantitative and qualitative standards produces results that can lead to modified objectives. Statistics to substantiate quantitative standards can be derived from:

1.   Usage statistics from automated circulation systems. These indicate frequency of materials use.

2.   Inventory figures. Resource turnover, loss and damage, and missing materials statistics indicate extent of use. Total materials count can substantiate materials per student criteria.

3.   Individual circulation logs. Such logs indicate the frequency of patron use of library materials and the types of materials used.

4.   Class scheduling log. Depending on the amount of data acquired when a visit is scheduled, several facts can be determined: proportion of staff and student body using materials and services; the frequency of use of specific resources or services; the age levels of users; specific subgroups being served; and subject matter preferences.

Evidence of meeting qualitative standards can be derived from:

1.   **Lesson plans.** Careful planning will reveal the frequency of use of resources and specific classroom objectives planned cooperatively with faculty. The plan should also specify the effectiveness with which the students achieved the lesson objectives.

2.   **Personnel evaluations.** Most districts have either formative evaluations, summative evaluations, or both for professional, para-professional, or non-professional staff. Student aides should receive educational credit for their services hours. Completion of specific skills and termination grades can provide both quantitative and qualitative data.

3.   **Surveys.** A systematic written evaluation should be conducted annually to obtain input from students, teachers and parents on the success of program objectives.

4.   **Conferences / Library Advisory Committee meetings.** Comments from faculty members and students can provide qualitative assessment of the value of the materials and services provided.

5.   **Criterion-referenced or teacher made tests**. These assessments can be used to evaluate student effectiveness in acquiring information skills or content area skills.

Skill 10.3   Utilize evaluation results to plan modifications to the library media program

The purposes of evaluation are to determine if all aspects of planning and implementation have been successfully accomplished. If evaluation shows unsuccessful outcomes, then the program must be modified. Successful outcomes can be used to confirm program objectives and to promote the media center programs.

Some strategies for the use of program evaluation include:

1.   To produce an annual report to be included in the school's annual report to parents or other publications for circulation in the community.
2.   To review and modify long-range goals and plan immediate changes in short-range goals.
3.   To lobby for budgetary or personnel support.
4.   To solicit assistance from faculty and administration in making curricular or instructional changes to maximize use of media center materials, equipment, and services.
5.   To plan greater involvement of students in academic and personal use of media center materials and services.

COMPETENCY 11.0 COMPREHENSION OF SKILLS REQUIRED TO PLAN, PREPARE, ADVOCATE, AND ADMINISTER A BUDGET

Skill 11.1 Identify methods for planning and preparing a library media budget based on patron needs and program goals and objectives

In preparation for constructing the budget for the school library media center, the school media professionals need to consider the following items:

1. The standards set by state departments of education, local school boards, and regional accreditation associations. Changes in standards sometimes necessitate changes in local budget planning.
2. The sources of funds that support the media center program.
3. The prioritized list of program goals and the cost of meeting these goals.

Determining the relationship between program goals and funding involve the study of

1. Past inventories and projections of future needs.
2. Quantitative and qualitative collection standards at all levels.
3. School and district curriculum plans.
4. Community needs.
5. Fiscal deadlines.

AASL/AECT provides guidelines for four factors in calculating the budget for the print and non-print collection: variation in student population, attrition by weeding, attrition by date, and attrition by loss. A formula for an estimated budget is then calculated based on points established for each of these factors. The estimation for replacement is figured on a base number of collection items required regardless of school size. The minimum collection standard is determined by the state or regional accreditation requirements.

Another method of estimating a budget for the print collection is based on the types of materials needed (e.g., replacement books, periodicals, books for growth and expansion, and reference books). It is recommended that 5% of the total books in the print collection be used in the formula.

Here is the recommended formula:

Replacement Cost = 5% x number of books x average cost of book

For periodicals, multiply the number of periodicals by the average subscription price.

Use the following figures to calculate book collection expansion:

- at 90% fulfillment of basic requirement, add 3%-5%;
- at 75%-90% fulfillment,
- use 10%-15%;
- and at less than 75%, use 15%-25%.

For reference books, multiply the number of sets times the average set price.

In a hypothetical school of 1000-1500 students, SAC recommends a base collection of 9200 volumes plus 5 volumes per student in excess of 1000 students (i.e., a minimum collection of 10,200 books). If that school has only 75% (7650 or fewer), the expansion formula should be

15-25% x existing collection x average book price.

If our hypothetical school has 7500 books, the formula might be

20% x 7500 x $20 = $30,000.

If the school has 75-90% of the recommended 10,200 books, one can meet expansion guidelines by adding 10-15% of the collection.

The formula would then be

10% x 8160 x $20 = $16,320.

Finally, if the school is at 90-100% of the recommendation, we expand by 3-5% or

5% x 9690 x $20 = $9690.

The SAC standard for periodicals is no fewer than 10 titles or one for each 25 students, whichever is greater; after the print subscriptions equal 30, the remaining requirement may be satisfied with non-print resources. For example, a school may have 50 print subscriptions and 2 non-print databases.
If the average print subscription price is $20 annually and the average non-print database is $2000, this school should estimate $5000 for periodicals.

If two sets of reference books at an average price of $1000 are needed, the estimated cost is $2000.

Calculations for audio-visual materials follow the same basic pattern.

Equipment estimations are based on multiplying four elements: the current inventory replacement value; replacement of lost, stolen, or damaged items; average age of the equipment; and the inflation rate. If a school hypothetically has a current value of $200,000, the average age of items is 5 years, the average replacement cost is $200, and the inflation rate is 1.3 percent, the equipment estimation would be calculated as follows:

$$\$200,000 \times 5 = \$1,000,000 \times .013 = 13,000 + \$200 = \$13,200$$

The total estimated collection budget then equals the sum of estimates. At 90% satisfaction of collection requirement, our total would be

$$\$9690 + \$5000 + \$2000 + \$13,200 = \$29,890$$

In districts in which the school library media center allocation is not calculated on local recommendations but on an across the board per capita figure, the school library media specialist must then work with the administration to secure necessary funds from the school budget. If funds are not categorized at the district level, the school library media specialist must then set a percentage for each category based on the previously discussed factors.

Having considered all factors, the budget process should parallel budget plans to the program goals and objectives. To achieve this correlation the process should follow these steps.

1. Communicate program and budget considerations to administration, faculty, student body and community groups, allowing sufficient time for input from all groups.
2. Work with representatives from all groups to finalize short- range objectives and review long-range goals for use of funds.
3. Build a system of flexible encumbrance and transfer of funds as changes in needs occur.
4. As part of the program promotion, communicate budgetary concerns to all interested parties.

Skill 11.2   Identify funding sources that support library media programs

Unlike public libraries, school library media centers are not usually the recipients of endowments or private gifts. Instead, school library media centers receive money from local and state tax dollars. The major portion of the funds comes from district allotments for instructional materials or capital outlay that are regulated by the state. Schools that have accreditation must adhere to regional guidelines that assure the accreditation. The funding formulas specifically used for school library media budgets vary from district to district but basically comply with the following regulations.

State:

1.   Local operation. In Florida, school boards have ultimate responsibility for district allocations. School library media centers funds are allocated from the district operating budget. The funds may be administered at the district or school level according to a per capita figure that is adequate to meet operation costs and contractual obligations.

2.   Regional guidelines. SAC produces an expenditures requirement based on student body size, allowing a school to average expenditures over a three-year period in which averaged expenditures do not fall below the standard.

3.   State funds provided by special legislation. Technology block grants have provided funds for retrofitting schools to create local area networks, wide-area networks, and telecommunications services.

Federal:

1.   Block grants included in federal education acts. Awarded to states or specific districts, these grants are limited in scope and time. They must be applied for on a competitive basis and renewal depends on the recipient's ability to prove that grant objectives have been met.

2.   Current federal funds are earmarked for innovative technologies, not operating costs.

In addition to official funding sources, there are other forms of assistance from the community that should be reflected in the budget plan. Because this assistance is in the form of service rather than real dollars, estimated values must be determined. Some community assistance includes

1.   Partnerships with local businesses. Free wiring from cable television companies, guest speakers, distance learning opportunities, and workshops in new technologies are just a few possible services.

2.   Education support groups. The education committee of the local Chamber of Commerce, a private education economic council, or parent associations may conduct fund-raisers or offer mini-grants.

Skill 11.3   Identify strategies that will effectively communicate budget needs

To ensure the budgetary needs of the school library media program are effectively communicated, it is important to involve staff, students, parents and community members in the planning and evaluation process. By evaluating the media program, needs are outlined. The evaluation findings will help the media specialist develop a plan for improvement, and this plan will assist in identifying funding needs.

Collaboration is the key to the evaluation process. The media specialist should work with the school to determine the instructional needs of staff and students. Present this data to the members of the media advisory committee and allow them to make budgetary decisions based on the information presented.
The specialist should also keep all staff members informed of his process, using staff or planning meetings to share information about library resources and needs.

The specialist should also invite parents and community members to be involved in the school library media program. Share with them the goals and objectives of the program as well as the resources that would meet student needs.

By sharing information with all parties that hold influence in the budget making process, the media specialist will assure that students, faculty, staff and community members understand the needs and importance of a well-funded library media program.

COMPETENCY 12.0 KNOWLEDGE OF PERSONAL PLANNING FOR THE LIBRARY MEDIA PROGRAM

Skill 12.1 Distinguish between professional responsibilities and paraprofessional activities

Professional responsibilities and activities are those outlined in the performance indicators throughout Competency 4. The school library media specialist has responsibility for developing program goals, collection development, budget management, consultation with teachers in using existing resources or producing new materials, provision for student instruction and staff development, and overseeing the paraprofessional and nonprofessional staffs.

The paraprofessional is a person qualified for a special area of media such as graphics, photography, instructional television, electronics, media production or computer technology. Often called a technical assistant, this person has training in his or her specialty and often holds an associate's or bachelor's degree in this specialty. While the paraprofessional may have some education training, he or she will most likely not have a bachelor's degree in library or information sciences, although some community colleges are now offering certificates in Library Assistantship.

The paraprofessional's responsibilities are in the areas of production, maintenance, and special services to students and teachers. Some of the paraprofessional's duties might include

1. Working with teachers in the design and production of media for classroom instruction.
2. Creating promotional materials and preparing special need media (e.g., video yearbook, audio or videotape duplication, preparation of materials for faculty meetings and staff development activities).
3. Operating and maintaining production equipment (e.g., laminator, Thermofax).
4. Maintaining computers and peripherals.
5. Evaluating media and equipment collection and recommending purchases.
6. Developing ways to use existing and emerging technologies.
7. Assisting teachers and students in locating and using media and equipment.
8. Repairing or making provisions for repair of materials and equipment.
9. Circulating equipment.
10. Maintaining records on circulation, maintenance, and repair of media and equipment.

The non-professional staff assumes responsibility for operational procedures (i.e., clerical, secretarial, technical, maintenance) that relieve the school library professional and paraprofessional of routine tasks so they can better perform their responsibilities.

Some specific nonprofessional activities include

1.   Conducting accounting and bookkeeping procedures.
2.   Unpacking, processing and shelving new materials.
3.   Processing correspondences, records, and manuals.
4.   Circulating materials and equipment.
5.   Assisting with materials production.
6.   Assisting with maintenance and repair of materials and equipment.
7.   Handling accounting procedures.
8.   Assisting with inventory.
9.   Assisting with services provided by electronic and computer equipment.

Skill 12.2   Evaluate the adequacy of a staffing plan for a library media program

Staffing plans should be evaluated against regional guidelines. The Southern Association of Colleges and Schools provides accreditation guidelines for K-12 schools including recommendations for school library media centers. For instance a school with 500–749 students should have one full time media specialist and four support staff for administration, media or technology. The accreditation guidelines account for schools of varying sizes, and the media specialist should refer to these when creating a staffing plan.

The number of students at a school can determine staffing numbers and positions as well as the increase of technology. While it is always important to have adequate technical support and media staff, resources are not infinite, and the library media specialist must examine and evaluate the responsibilities of current staff members in order to identify whether additional assistance is necessary. One method would be to have each staff member complete a time analysis for a week or so. This allows the specialist to compare the results from this to the actual job description, using his or her findings to identify staffing needs within the media program. Outside evaluators can also be effective in determining needs.

Skill 12.3   Identify appropriate methods to instruct, supervise, and evaluate library media staff

The diversity of user needs, school enrollments and school/district support services are some factors that affect staff size. Oftentimes, the duties of staff members at different levels can overlap, only differing in the amount of decision-making and accountability.

If the school places a high priority on an efficient library media center program, there should be a minimum of two full-time professionals, one paraprofessional and two nonprofessionals, one to function as an office manager and one as a technical assistant. In 1976, *Florida School Library Media Programs: A Guide for Excellence* recommended minimum staff based on student enrollment. Any school from 500-999 should have two library media specialists and one full-time support person. From 1000-1499, there should be two media specialists and two support persons. Schools with student bodies from 1500-1999 should have three full-time media specialists.

However, ALA and NEA standards for School Media Programs recommended two support staff for each specialist in any school with under 2000 enrollment. SAC Standards recommend that in a school with two specialists on staff, two paraprofessionals may be hired in lieu of an additional professional. Unfortunately, when schools are looking to save money, the support staff are usually the first to be sacrificed.

When the support staff is reduced, the media specialist must assume operational duties which detract from his or her professional responsibilities. Volunteers can help with circulation and supplemental tasks that reflect their unique talents and experiences, but they should never be used as substitutes for paid clerical and technical staff. Student assistants, like volunteers, may be trained to assist the media specialist but should not be given duties that are the responsibilities of paid nonprofessionals. Students might assist with production of materials, maintenance of the decoration and physical appearance of the center, instruction in materials location, use of electronic/computer databases, and shelving books and periodicals. It is recommended that student aides be given course credit or certificates of achievement to reward them for their services.

When working with nonprofessional staff, volunteers, and student assistants, the specialist should realize that those who are not trained as support staff will need to be trained on the job. Here are several strategies for training these individuals:

1. Using the district's job description and evaluation instrument for the particular position, prioritizing skills and responsibilities in order from greatest to least immediacy.
2. Determining the individual's knowledge and mastery of skills by observing performance.
3. Planning a systematic training of remaining skills to be addressed one at a time.

The supervision of media professionals is the responsibility of an administrator, and the supervision of support staff is the responsibility of the head library media specialist (if that position is administrative) or of an administrator who receives input from the media specialist. Periodic oral evaluations and annual written evaluations using the appropriate instrument should be conducted for each media staff member. These evaluations should result in suggestions for training or personal development.

Studies conducted in recent years show that there is a personnel crisis in Florida's school media centers, especially in elementary schools. In an article in *Florida Media Quarterly*, Yahn and Townsend recommended that as many as three different positions—instructional specialist, technology specialist and media technician—be added to each school's staff in order to properly use the technologies for which Florida's Incentive Block Grants have provided.

COMPETENCY 13.0 KNOWLEDGE OF POLICIES AND COMPREHENSION OF PROCEDURES USED IN THE LIBRARY MEDIA PROGRAM

Skill 13.1 Distinguish between a policy and procedure

A policy is the written statement of principle in which the policy-making agency guarantees a management practice or course of action that is expedient and consistent. A procedure is the course of action taken to execute the policy. In government, legislation is policy and law enforcement is procedure.

Educational policy makers include Congress and state legislatures, state and local school boards, national library media organizations and school library media program managers. Policies adopted at the local level must support both district school board policies and state laws. Regulations concerning certification, state budget allocations and standards for selecting and approving state-adopted instructional materials are developed at the state level.

Matters such as collection development and responding to challenges of materials are usually set at district level. Local issues such as hours of operation, circulation of materials and equipment, and personnel supervision are set by the appropriate school policy makers for library media.

Procedures for administering district and state policies are usually determined by usual practice or local precedence. Procedures for specific administration tasks such as determining budget categories, expending funds, maintaining collection size should be clearly stated in a school library media procedures manual.

Certification, state budget, state adopted materials → State

hours, circulation, supervision → school

wanting a book pulled from library → district

Skill 13.2   Identify district policies that impact the school library media program

The two basic sources for district policies are school board rules and the procedures manual from district media services offices. Information provided in these documents should be reviewed before any school level planning is done.

It is also necessary to know which policies and procedures are the responsibility of the district and which ones are the responsibility of the school. For example, school boards are charged with the responsibility to set propriety standards for selection of instructional materials. However, school boards do not select the texts or library books for individual schools. Procedures for implementing propriety standards are determined at each school site based on the needs of its students.

School boards may set policy for a challenge and identify a procedure for its sequential investigation. As a defender of intellectual freedom and a trained educator, the school library media specialist should have the latitude to recommend and purchase quality materials. He or she should also be prepared to substantiate those purchases in terms of readability, social appropriateness, and artistic quality.

In terms of professional development, school districts are bound by law to maintain a properly certified staff, but it is the obligation of the employee to learn what and where professional development activities are available, to take six course credits within the five-year period, and to submit proof of same to the certification officer prior to the June 30 deadline in the renewal year.

Operational procedures also change from district-to-district. Some counties have centralized reprographics facilities; therefore, district policies are set for reproduction of materials that comply with copyright laws and district procedures for formatting, according to the type of equipment used, are spelled out in a printed manual which should be available at all school sites.
Some counties have centralized materials processing so that classification and cataloging procedures are administered at the county level.

copyright → district

Skill 13.3   Identify the participants and their roles in developing school library media policies, procedures, and rules

Every member of the school community has a different perspective on the learning environment. Because of this, it is always preferable to develop and evaluate local policies and procedures with the aid of a library advisory committee. Here are the various perspectives that community members can bring to the committee meetings.

Participants	Role
Administrator	clarifies school vision and goals.
Media specialist	identifies factors such as time, personnel, resources and budget that affect school goals.
Teacher	identifies media center resources and services that correlate with instruction.
Student	identifies materials and activities that fulfill learning needs.
Parents (Optional)	identify avenues of communication with parents and community.

Once the advisory committee has formulated acceptable policies and procedures, the district director and/or directors of elementary and secondary instruction should review and provide input before adoption.

Skill 13.4   Evaluate the components of a school library media procedures manual

Constant evaluation is necessary to determine the effectiveness of a school library media procedures manual. Items to consider during the evaluation process are as follows:

- Do the procedures outline the most efficient methods for completing the task?
- Do the policies and procedures reflect the principles of the library profession with regards to intellectual freedom, copyright, and the rights of all users?
- Do the policies and procedures promote and enhance student learning?
- Do the policies and procedures provide equitable access to resources?
- Do the policies and procedures provide maximum access to resources?
- Do the policies and procedures promote responsible use of resources?
- Do the policies and procedures comply with national, state, and local guidelines?

Answers to these questions will assist a library media specialist in honing and revising a library media procedures manual.

Skill 13.5   Identify methods of communicating school library media policies, procedures and rules

The most efficient method of communicating policies and procedures to the faculty is the library media procedures manual. This manual should first present the mission and long-range objectives and then the specific policies designed to meet these objectives. Specific procedures for using the resources and services should include scheduling of the facility, circulation of materials and equipment, requests for consultation or instruction, and requests for production of media.

Communicating policies to students is best facilitated by a structured orientation program and frequent visits to the media center to practice applying those procedures. In schools with closed circuit television, a live or taped program concerning library media use can be very successful.

COMPETENCY 14.0   KNOWLEDGE OF LIBRARY MEDIA SPACE UTILIZATION

Skill 14.1   Identify the elements of an effective library media facilities arrangement

Since the arrangement of a library media facility assures a welcoming and productive learning environment for staff, students, and community members, the media specialist should take heed of the following recommendations.

1.   Flexibility of arrangement ensures that the facility can be easily modified as resources and service needs change. Traffic flow should provide easy, logical access to all spaces.
2.   A realistic assessment of security needs will provide for material detection systems, alarms or locks to protect electronic equipment, and convenient placement of communications devices.
3.   Proper placement of electrical outlets, fire extinguishers, smoke detectors, and thermostats ensures safety for users and convenience for the staff.
4.   Provision must be made for the physically impaired to have barrier-free access to the center and its resources.
5.   All areas requiring supervision should be readily visible from other areas of the center.
6.   There should be a carefully planned relationship of spaces used for supporting activities and services.

The specifics of spatial arrangement depend upon the types and quantities of resources and services provided. New school design should place the media center in a central location that is easily accessible to all academic areas. Within the center itself the following spatial arrangement factors should be addressed.

1.   A large central area for reading, listening, viewing, and computing, which has ready access to materials and equipment. AASL/AECT guidelines recommend that this main seating area be 25%-75% of the total square footage allocation, depending on program requirements. Forty square feet should be allotted per student user. Within this area or peripheral to it should be smaller areas that provide for independent study or accommodate students with physical impairments. Seating should be adequate to accommodate the number of users during peak hours. SAC guidelines recommend floor space and seating to accommodate 10% of the student body, but the media center should not be expected to seat fewer than 40 or more than 100 students at one time.

between 40 - 100 seats

2.	Areas for small or medium-sized group activities. These areas may be acoustically special spaces adjacent to the central seating area or conference rooms, computer labs, or storytelling space. AASL/AECT recommends 1-3 areas or approximately 150 square feet with ample electrical outlets, good lighting and acoustics, and a wall screen.

3.	Space to house and display the collection. Materials that can be circulated outside the center should be easily accessible from the main seating area. Index tools should be highly visible and in the immediate proximity to the collections they index. A supervised circulation desk with easy access to non-circulable databases (i.e., periodicals, CD- ROM disks, microform, and videotape collections) should be close to the center's main entrance. AASL/AECT recommends a minimum of 400 square feet for stacks with an additional 200 foot allowance per 500 additional students.

4.	A reference materials area within or adjacent to the central seating area. The recommended area allowance is part of the total allotted for the stacks.

5.	Space for a professional collection and work area where the faculty and media professionals can work privately. T his area should be approximately 1 square foot per student.

6.	Administrative offices, with areas for resource and equipment processing, materials duplication and business materials storage. An area no smaller than 200 square feet should be available for offices alone and double that area if in-house processing is done.

7.	Equipment storage and circulation area close to administrative offices and with access to outside corridor. Space for maintenance and repair is optional depending on available staff to attend to these duties. This space should be no less than 400 square feet for storage with another 150 square feet if repair facilities are necessary.

8.	A media production area with space and equipment for production of audio and videotaping, graphics design, photography, computer programming and photocopying. (In some secondary schools, a dark room is included. Other schools with commercial photography classes and a full photography lab may seek services through the photography teacher.) This area may be as small as 50 square feet or as large as 700 square feet in a school with 500 students depending on the amount of equipment required to suit media production needs; in a school with 1000 or more students, at least 700-900 square feet should be allotted for media production.

9.   A television production studio for formal TV production class instruction and preparing special programming. Space for distribution of closed circuit programs and satellite transmissions should also be provided. A 1600 square foot studio (preferably 40' x 40' x 15') should be available whenever television classes are taught or studio videotaping is a program priority. AASL/AECT guidelines allow alternatives, namely for studio space available at the district for the use of students or mini-studios/portable videotape units where videotaping is done on a small scale.

10.   A large multi-purpose room adjacent to the media center is recommended, but optional in many schools. AASL/AECT recommends that this room be 700-900 square feet (i.e., classroom size) in a school with 500 students or 900-1200 square feet in a school with 1000 students. This room should be equipped for making all types of media presentations.

Skill 14.2   Identify factors that affect the school library media center atmosphere

Because of the diversity of services provided in a modern school library media center, it is important to foster a user-friendly atmosphere, one in which the patron is not only welcomed as a user of resources but is also involved as a producer of ideas and materials.

In considering the academic and personal needs of the user, the library media center should provide an atmosphere in which users can attain both basic skills and enrichment goals.

Here are several factors that influence the atmosphere of a library media center:

1.   Proximity to academic classes.
2.   Aesthetic appearance.
3.   Acoustical ceilings and floor coverings.
4.   Adequate temperature control.
5.   Adequate, non-glare lighting with controls for different types of viewing activities.
6.   Comfortable, appropriately sized, and durable furnishings.
7.   Diverse, plentiful, and current resources that are attractive to handle as well as easy to use.
8.   Courteous, helpful personnel, using supervisory techniques that encourage self-exploration and creativity while protecting the rules of library etiquette.

COMPETENCY 15.0 COMPREHENSION OF METHODS AND RESOURCES FOR ORGANIZING COLLECTIONS

Skill 15.1 Identify classification systems and purposes for using them

Two classification systems are prevalent in the United States.

1. The Library of Congress System uses a system which has been adopted by many colleges and universities since the 1960's.
2. The Dewey Decimal System is used predominately in schools and public libraries.

The purpose of both systems is to provide universal standards of organizing collections. These systems facilitate location of materials within a collection and enable institutions to share information and materials that are uniformly grouped.

Skill 15.2 Identify the fields of a bibliographic record

The MARC format is relatively universal and enables a school library to utilize many commercial automation tools. The format allows for unlimited fields which provide more efficient cataloging for both print and non-print items. Each field is marked with a tag. A tag represents a specific piece of information, i.e., 245 tag lists title information, and the 520 tag marks the summary.

The MARC format assists in preserving bibliographic integrity. Bibliographic integrity refers to the accuracy and uniformity with which items are catalogued. Following a standard set of international rules, *Anglo-American Cataloguing Rules*, enables users to locate materials equally well in all libraries that subscribe to these rules. To maintain this integrity, catalogers

1. Recognize an International Standard Bibliographic Description (ISBD) that establishes the order in which bibliographic elements will appear in catalog entries.
2. Note changes that occur after each five years review of ISBD.
3. Agree to catalog all materials using the AACR standards.

The components of a basic bibliographic record (may be used in LCC or DDC shelf-list cards or in OCLC's MARC records for automated systems):

1. Call Number. Includes DDC or LCCN classification number followed by a book identification identifier (numerals or letters).
2. Author Main Entry Heading. Use name by which author is most commonly known even if that name is a pseudonym.
3. Title and Statement of Responsibility Area. Include title, subtitle, or parallel titles and name(s) of authors, editors, illustrators, translators, or groups functioning in authorship capacity.
4. Edition Statement. Provide ordinal number of edition.
5. Material Specific Details. Used with only four materials (computer files, cartographic materials, printed music, and serials in all formats).
6. Publication and Distribution Area. Include place of publication, name of publisher and copyright date.
7. Physical Description Area. Include the extent of the work (number of pages, volumes, or other units); illustrative matter; size/dimensions; and accompanying materials.
8. Series. Provide title of series and publication information if different from statement of responsibility.
9. Notes. Provide information to clarify any other descriptive components, including audio-visual formats or reading levels.
10. Standard numbers. Provide ISBN, ISSN, or LCC number, price, or other terms of availability.

It is necessary for all entries to have standardized subject headings. *Sear's List of Subject Headings* is generally used in Dewey Decimal classification, while the Library of Congress has its own subject heading list.

Skill 15.3   Identify sources for obtaining bibliographic information

Many companies that serve libraries provide a service that provides complete MARC records for materials ordered. This is a time-saving feature for school library media specialists that would have to hand key in all of the MARC tags. The primary way of determining use of library materials and services is to examine circulation records. With automated systems it is possible to generate monthly statistics on the number of items circulated. Dividing by the average number of items a user may check out during that circulation period will provide an idea of the number of users who visited the media center.

Most school libraries use an automated circulation system that requires information to be cataloged in MARC format. MARC stands for Machine Readable Cataloging. If we break down the term, machine readable means that a machine such as a computer can read the content of the record. The cataloging record provides details about an item such as the description, main entry, subjects, and classification or call number. Cataloging records follow specific rules as outlined in AACR2 (Anglo-American Cataloging Rules, Second Edition).

There are three levels of bibliographic description.

1. Level 1 descriptions are the simplest and most appropriate for small or general collections. Although they satisfy AACR standards, they are not considered full records.
2. Level 2 descriptions are more detailed and are used by medium to large libraries where clients use materials for research. Many libraries, including small media centers, use description format somewhere between Level 1 and Level 2.
3. Level 3 descriptions are full records that require application of every AACR rule. Most major libraries, even the Library of Congress, develop some system just short of full Level 3 cataloging.

OCLC bibliographic records (MARC) use both a short form (Level I enhanced) and a long form (Level 2).

Skill 15.4 Apply standardized techniques to maintain bibliographic integrity

Bibliographic integrity refers to the accuracy and uniformity with which items are catalogued. Following a standard set of international rules, *Anglo-American Cataloguing Rules*, enables users to locate materials equally well in all libraries that subscribe to these rules. To maintain this integrity, catalogers

1. Recognize an International Standard Bibliographic Description (ISBD) that establishes the order in which bibliographic elements will appear in catalog entries.

2. Note changes that occur after each five years review of ISBD.

3. Agree to catalog all materials using the AACR standards.

COMPETENCY 16.0 KNOWLEDGE OF METHODS FOR PROMOTING THE LIBRARY MEDIA PROGRAM

Skill 16.1 Select methods of identifying users and nonusers of the school library media program

In elementary schools where whole classes visit on a regular schedule, usage may be tabulated by multiplying class size by the number of visits. In schools with flexible scheduling, keeping a log of visits and the number of participants in each group might result in a truer figure since users may do in-house research, use computers, create media productions, or otherwise use services that do not involve borrowing materials.

Skill 16.2 Identify techniques to attract and retain school library media users

Libraries have changed from the stuffy no-talking zones of the past to bright, interactive, and frequently noisy epicenters of information at the heart of many schools. It is the job of the media specialist to encourage library use and to actively market the library to new and existing users. These users may include but are not limited to staff, administrators, students, parents, and support staff.

Marketing materials may take the form of posters, flyers, newsletters, bulletin boards, signs, and e-mail notifications. In this day of budget shortfalls and the mistaken impression that the Internet is the end all, be all for finding information, the role of the media center in prompting lifelong student learning is often taken for granted, overlooked, or ignored.

It is important to:
- Make users aware of new technology or resources available within the library.
- Schedule classes, workshops, games, and continuing education for users.
- Coordinate with teachers so students are recognized or offered extra credit for properly using library resources.

To the best of your ability, have adequate staff on hand to answer questions with limited or no waiting. Offer frequent encouragement and advice to library patrons and don't wait for them to come to you. Rather, do walk around where you ask each individual how they're getting along and if they need help with a search. Identify the most commonly used resources and make them readily available for easy access. Anticipates user needs by listening to what students and staff say they want from their library. Work the teachers to integrate as much as possible the programs of your media center into the curriculum.

Skill 16.3   Identify techniques to promote and elicit support for the library media program

Establish and nurture an administrative partnership with the principal and district director of media to develop, establish, and fund library program goals. In larger districts that have a district director of media, avenues of support may be clearly defined. In smaller districts, where the media director also handles other administrative duties or where there is no district coordinator, support is based on the lobbying efforts of the school library media specialist. In any case, the principal must be the media center's staunchest ally. Present the annual program goals and implementation procedures to the principal early in the school year for his input and approval. Invite him to participate in faculty inservices and advisory committee meetings. Ask to be included on the school's curriculum planning team.

Exhibit your willingness to assume a leadership role in integrating the library media program into the total school program. Make every attempt to ensure that some phase of the library media program appears in each year's school improvement plan.

Work with the district media director and other school library media specialists to establish and maintain a uniformly excellent district library media program. Continually evaluate the goals and objectives of the school program compared to the district program and matched to the users' needs as identified in annual assessments.

Attend school board meetings. Be aware of all issues affecting the media program, instruction, and the budget. Invite county or area superintendents and school board members to district media meetings to discuss issues and plan improvements. Make yourself and your enthusiasm for the library media program visible.

Read widely in the resources listed in 1.3. A knowledgeable library media specialist is the best human resource in the school. There is perhaps no better promotion for the media center than having students, teachers, and administrators seeking information from the library media center staff.

Attend college courses, inservice training, and professional conferences. Offer to teach night college courses, supervise a library media candidate, offer workshops for school faculty, and make presentations at conferences. However, remember to be selective. Never forsake your ethical responsibility to serve patrons by overextending your commitments.

Keep apprised of state certification requirements for certificate renewal and complete renewal requirements (1.9) in a timely manner.

Systematically assess program needs at least annually. Always have available statistics about media center use (5.1), lesson plans or visitation schedules, and written evaluations of instructional activities. Make presentations to School Improvement Committees, parent support groups, or community agencies. Making thorough, accurate reports indicates a well-managed program and encourages maximum support.

COMPETENCY 17.0   KNOWLEDGE OF POLICIES AND PROCEDURES FOR COLLECTION DEVELOPMENT

Skill 17.1   Identify the elements of a collection development policy

Each school library media center should develop a policy tailored to the philosophy and objectives of that school's educational program. This policy provides guidelines by which all participants in the selection process can get insight into their responsibilities. The policy statement should reflect the following factors.

1.   Compatibility with district, state, regional, and national guidelines (see Skill 1.2).
2.   Adherence to the principles of intellectual freedom and the specifics of copyright law.
3.   Recognition of the rights of individuals or groups to challenge policies, procedures or selected items, and the establishment of procedures for dealing fairly with such challenges.
4.   Recognition of users needs and interests, including community demographics.

The policy should include the school library media center's mission and the criteria used in the selection process. General criteria for the selection of all media include:

1.   **Authenticity**. Media should be accurate, current, and authoritative. Copyright or printing dates are indicators of currency, but examination of content is often necessary to determine the relevance of the subject matter to its intended use. Research into the reputations of contributors and comparison to other materials by the same producer will provide insight into its literary quality.

2.   **Appropriateness of Subject Matter**. Consider suitability to the school's educational objectives, scope of coverage, treatment and arrangement of content, importance of content to the user, and appropriateness to users' ability levels and learning styles.

3.   **Appeal.** Consideration of the artistic quality and language appropriateness will help in the selection of media that students will enjoy using. Properly selected materials should stimulate creativity and inspire further learning.

Authenticity
Appropriateness
Appeal

Skill 17.2   Identify the characteristics of a collection development plan

As the specialist continually evaluates the items in the collection, he or she should also focus on these various elements of a collection development plan:

1. Knowledge of the existing collection or the ability to create a new collection.
2. Knowledge of the external environment of the media center, including the school and the community.
3. Assessment of school programs and user needs.
4. Development of overall policies and procedures.
5. Guidelines for specific selection decisions.
6. Evaluation criteria.
7. Establishment of a process for planning and implementing the collection plan.
8. Establishment of acquisition policies and procedures.
9. Establishment of maintenance program.
10. Establishment of procedures for evaluating the collection.

After recognizing these elements, the specialist should follow the following procedures for implementing the plan:

1. Learn the collection. A library media specialist, new to a school with an existing collection, should use several approaches to becoming familiar with the collection.
   a. Browse the shelves. Note your degree of familiarity with titles. Examine items that are unfamiliar to you. Determine the relationship between the materials on similar subjects in different formats. Include the reference and professional collections in your browse. Consider the accessibility of various media and the ease with which they can be located by users.
   b. Locate the center's procedures manual. Determine explanations for any seeming irregularities in the collection.
   c. Determine if any portions of the collection are housed in areas outside the media center.

If the library media specialist is required to create a new collection, he or she should
   a. Consult with the district director about new school collection policies.
   b. Examine the collections of other comparable schools.
   c. Examine companies, like Baker and Taylor's, who establish new collections based on criteria provided by the school.

2. Learn about the community.
   a. Examine the relationship of the media center to the total school program and other information agencies.
   b. Become familiar with the school, cultural, economic and political characteristics of the community and their influence on the schools.

3. Study the school's curriculum and the needs of the users (students and faculty). Examine the proportions of basic skills to enrichment offerings, academic or vocational courses, and requirements and electives.
   a. Determine the ability levels and grouping techniques for learners.
   b. Determine instructional objectives of teachers in various content areas or grade levels.

4. Examine existing policies and procedures for correlation to data acquired in researching the school and community.

5. Examine specific selection procedures to determine if guidelines are best met.

6. Examine evaluation criteria for effectiveness in maintaining an appropriate collection.

7. Examine the process to determine that accurate procedures are in place to meet the criteria.

8. Examine the acquisition plan. Determine the procedure by which materials are ordered, received, paid for and processed.

9. Examine maintenance procedures for repairing or replacing materials and equipment, replacing consumables, and discarding non-repairable items.

10. Examine the policies and procedures for evaluation, then examine the collection itself to determine if policies and procedures are contributing to quality and quantity.

Procedures for maintaining the collection are perhaps the most important in the collection plan. The plan itself must provide efficient, economical procedures for keeping materials and equipment in usable condition.

Maintenance policies for equipment and some policies for materials are determined at the district level. Procedures to satisfy these policies are followed at the building level.

1. Replacement or discard of damaged items based on comparison of repair to replacement cost. Districts usually maintain repair contracts with external contractors for major repairs that cannot be done at the school or district media service center.

2. Equipment inventory and records on repair or disposal. Usage records help with the transfer of usable items from school to school

Policies and procedures for periodic inspection, preventive maintenance and cleaning, and minor repairs are established and conducted at the school media center.

1. Print material. Spine and jacket repairs, taping torn pages and replacing processing features.
2. Non-print materials. Cleaning, splicing, and repairing cases.
3. Equipment. Repairing broken equipment, handling technical issues, cleaning, replacement.
4. Inventory and weeding of print and non-print materials; regular replacement of worn or outdated equipment.
5. Record-keeping on items that have been lost or stolen, damaged by nature or neglect, or transferred/discarded.
6. Security systems operation, procedures for emergency disasters, and safe storage of duplicate records.

Skill 17.3   Identify the relationship between district collection development policy and school collection development plans

District collection development policies may be general or specific, but they should always address areas of concern to all schools. The policy statement should reflect the philosophy of the district, indicate the legal responsibility of the school board, and delegate of authority to specific individuals at the district and school level. One statement will usually address all instructional materials, including textbook and library media resources.

Here are some objectives which might be included in the policy:

1. To provide resources that contain information about supporting and enhancing the school's curriculum.
2. To provide resources that satisfy user needs, abilities, and learning styles.
3. To provide resources that develop literary appreciation and artistic values.
4. To provide resources that reflect the culture and ethnic diversity of society and the contributions of members of various groups to our country's heritage.
5. To provide materials that enable students to solve problems and make judgments relevant to real life.
6. To provide resources that present opposing views on historical or contemporary issues so that students may learn to think critically and objectively.

District plans may deal with the following areas:

1. Funding policies.
   a. **Allocation**. School media centers generally receive a portion of the general operating budget. The total amount is determined by a per student dollar amount and may come directly from the district media accounts or, under school-based management, may be apportioned from school budget categories.
   b. **Authorization for purchases**. These policies vary depending on who has control of the budget (e.g., principal, district or media supervisor, district purchasing agent or any combination of the three). In some districts purchase requests must also be approved by curriculum supervisors.
   c. **Supplemental sources**. Federal or state block grants, endowments, or district capital outlay funds are allocated on a per capita or special project allotment basis. Responsibility for preparation of grant applications is supervised or conducted at the district level. Some districts also set policy concerning the suitability of private donations of material or property items.

2. Preview of considered materials. Some districts seek total control of previewing.

3. Collection size. Districts will frequently set minimum materials and equipment levels, especially if they aim to meet SAC accreditation standards. SAC standard 5.4.1 specifies a minimum book collection which is approximately 10 volumes per student. Responsibility for start-up collections at new schools are governed by district media.

4. Resource sharing. Some decisions in regards to delivery systems, cooperative funding, software licensing, and liability are district determined.

5. Time constraints. All districts require that funds be expended by a specific deadline.

6. District media library policies and procedures. Materials that are too expensive for school budgets and will be used by more than one school are maintained at the district library.

7. Equipment and materials maintenance and repair policy. Districts maintain repair contracts and set procedures for their use. Annual inventories, especially of equipment, are required and periodic assessment of policies are conducted.

8. Central processing. Available in some districts, this department processes materials for convenience and uniformity.

Skill 17.4   Identify criteria for evaluating and selecting all forms of media, hardware, and equipment

In addition to the general selection criteria, certain other specific criteria must be imposed when selecting media and equipment. Types of media include:

1.   Printed or display media (pamphlets, handouts, flannel boards, flip charts etc.).
2.   Overhead transparencies.
3.   Slides and filmstrips.
4.   Audiotape recordings.
5.   Videotape recordings.
6.   Computer software.
7.   CD-ROM and laser disks.

Some or all criteria may be applied to the media formats:

1.   **Technical quality**. The sound quality, picture focus, font size, screen color, and physical dimensions must be technically correct and artistically appealing for the information within to be appreciated and absorbed by the learner.

2.   **Packaging**. Non-print media need to be packaged in reusable containers if they are to be circulated and protected from wear and tear.

3.   **Cost**. The advantages of one format over another must be studied for the limits of the current budget, the size of the group to be served, and the durability of the product in terms of the investment. Some products may be considered for rental rather than purchase.

4.   **Applicability**. The product should be suitable for available equipment to use it with, appropriate to the climate and environment in which it will be used, and potentially usable with individuals as well as small or large groups.

5.   **Educational value**. If possible, the product advertisement should provide evidence that the selected media format has been tested with learners to prove its value to the learning process.

Besides the criteria for evaluating formats, a media specialist should also evaluate possible equipment with the following criteria in mind:

1.   **Balance**. The amount of audio-visual materials, the frequency of need for these materials, and the preference of teachers will influence the number of items to purchase. District guidelines may set minimum levels.

2.   **Condition**. Some years the budget may need to take into consideration the need for replacing worn or damaged pieces of equipment in the collection. Some new equipment is essential to keep up with new media formats.

When looking to add, replace, or repair equipment, remember these resources:

1.   Company catalogs.
2.   State or district approved lists.
3.   Services for free or reduced cost products: ITV, MECC.
4.   Preview or observation of products.

Skill 17.5   Identify sources that provide current information for selecting all forms of media, hardware, and equipment

Selection of equipment often depends upon the companies represented on the state bid list or local companies with whom the district contracts. Whenever shopping off the bid list, it is advisable to consult the district purchasing agent, as he or she may be able to secure better prices than those quoted in company catalogs. Company catalogs cite specifications of physical dimensions, power needs, and other technical capabilities and requirements. To review the quality and performance of the equipment, the media specialist can consult several periodicals, including *New Media, Technology Review, PC Week, MAC Week, Media and Methods.* He or she can also consult with other media professionals.

A number of resources may be used in the selection of print and non-print media.

1.   Catalogs from publishers and vendors.

2.   Bibliographies in outstanding reference books or text books.

3.   Lists provided by library associations such as *Selected Films for Young Adults* and *Outstanding Books for the College Bound.*

4.   Standard catalogs, including *Children's Catalog, Elementary School Library Collections* and *Senior High School Library Catalog*

5.   Lists of award winners, such as the Caldecott and Newbery awards.

6.   Lists of notable materials in books on children's literature (e.g., Pillon and Sutherland) and library media publications like the *School Library Media Annual*

Skill 17.6 **Identify selection tools for a specific need and apply selection criteria to determine whether a given resource should be included in a collection**

The following includes two examples of ways in which specific criteria may be applied.

1. A secondary science teacher has made a request for a microbiology book that is more readable for introductory or fundamental biology students. Direct examination of existing books reveals that they are all on an advanced reading level. The media specialist should

    a. Search available catalogs and materials lists and consult catalogs of other schools (SUNLINK).

    b. Validate the credentials of the producers of these titles.

    c. Determine the accuracy of content and the currency of the information. It may be necessary to preview requests for direct examination of copies available from publishers or in other collections.

    d. Determine cost, aesthetic appeal, durability of the product, and potential use by other science students.

    e. Solicit comments from teachers and students during the preview process.

    f. Present a list of titles and let the requesting teacher make selection(s).

2. A Pre-K class is added to an elementary school. The media specialist has the responsibility of securing materials appropriate to the younger users. The media specialist should

    a. Determine the learning needs of 3 and 4 year olds, consult with PK-teachers and media specialists in schools with existing PK collections, and use catalogs and other selection tools to construct a list of possible purchases.

    b. Compare cost of materials to product durability and quantity needed. For instance, cloth books, learning kits, and puppets may have greater initial cost, but these items may last longer.

    c. Factor in accessibility policies and storage limitations. Products purchased with media funds may be best stored in the PK classroom rather than circulated from the media center.

    d. Produce a list of recommended materials for committee review and approval.

Skill 17.7 **Identify strategies for assuring that the collection meets the current needs of students and staff**

Collection evaluation is necessary to determine responsiveness to the school program and instructional needs, access to materials outside the school, preferred user content and formats, and the efficiency of satisfying the media program.

Any or all the following procedures may provide data used to measure a collection's value.

1. The comparison of holdings records to bibliographies or catalogs of recommended titles.

2. The comparison of holdings records to lists of specific content or materials based on age or ability.

3. Direct examination of the collection to determine size, scope, and depth of the general collection or specific areas of the collection. This method also determines the principal condition of materials.

4. Circulation statistics indicate the popularity and frequency of use of certain segments of the collection. Large holdings of materials that do not circulate indicate a need for a policy change. As user needs change, it is necessary to weed materials that have no further application or that have lost their appeal.

5. User opinions, determined from surveys, interviews, or the nature of research being conducted, indicate changes in collection selection. Direct requests from teachers may also be solicited.

6. Consideration of standards and their applications as provided by professional library organizations, state departments of education, and regional accreditation commissions.

Skill 17.8 **Identify methods of communicating policies and procedures for collection development**

See Skill 13.5

COMPETENCY 18.0 KNOWLEDGE OF REQUIREMENTS FOR CIRCULATING AND MAINTAINING RESOURCES

Skill 18.1 Identify the components of a circulation plan that assures accessibility to resources

Circulation policies and procedures should be flexible to allow ready access and secure to protect borrowers' rights of confidentiality.

The components of circulation procedures include:

1.   A circulation system. Whether manual or automated, this system should
   a.   be simple to use for convenience of staff and the efficiency of borrowing,
   b.   provide for the loan and retrieval of print and non-print materials and equipment,
   c.   and facilitate the collection of circulation statistics.
2.   Rules governing circulation.
   a.   Length of loan period.
   b.   Process for handling overdues.
   c.   Limitations.
      i.   Number of items circulable to individual borrower.
      ii.   Overnight loan for special items (vertical file materials, reference books, audio-visual materials or equipment).
      iii.   Reserve collections.
3.   Rules governing fines for damages or lost materials.
4.   Security provisions.
   a.   Theft detection devices on print and non-print media.
   b.   Straps or lock-downs on equipment transported by cart.

Skill 18.2   Identify the collection and facilities preparation required to implement an automated library management system

To prepare to convert to an automated library management system there are three main categories that must be considered. The first is the budget, the next includes the technical considerations needed for automation, and the other is the data conversion.

• budget

• tech needed

• data conversion

The options available during the conversion process are often determined by the funds available. Necessary purchases would include the software, a barcode scanner for checkout, necessary hardware upgrades, and technical support. Other options could include a web-based searching option for home use and and the conversion of records by outside contractors. It is good to have a well-defined plan before beginning the process. When in doubt, the specialist should take small steps and increase as time and money allows.

Technical considerations fall into the software, hardware and infrastructure categories. When selecting software for library management, check local or state recommendations before making any decisions. The platform should match the computer systems most prevalent in your district. If your school is predominantly MAC-based then use a MAC platform; if Windows, use Windows. Before purchasing the software, make sure the computers in the school will support the requirements of the software and that the network infrastructure is in place to provide maximum access. District technical support staff should be able to assist with these decisions. It will be important to purchase or make sure that technical support is provided for the automation software manufacturer. This may involve an extra expense but will be money well spent, especially during the initial setup phase.

After the technical requirements are in place, it is time to begin the data conversion process. Transferring the current card catalog into electronic format can be a daunting job. It helps first to thoroughly weed the collection. By weeding, time is saved by not converting titles that will be discarded.

The actual conversion of information to electronic format will be the most time consuming task. Options include inputting the data onsite or hiring a company to convert the shelflist to electronic format, and the size of the budget is generally the biggest factor when making this choice. If the choice is to convert onsite, a wise investment would be the purchase of MARC CD-ROMS. This will make the specific process will speed up the task. Then again, there are companies who will convert the shelflist to MARC format for a rather minimal charge considering the time it takes to enter everything by hand. The specialist should explore the possibilities of utilizing such services and determine the impact on the automation budget.

Once the shelflist has been converted to electronic format, the books must be barcoded. This generally involves printing barcode stickers and placing them on each and every book. Volunteers and student helpers can make this process move quickly.

Next, all patron information needs to be added into the automated system. This can often be conducted by importing data from the school's attendance management system. If not, information will need to be keyed in by hand. Once all of the information is in, then the school library media specialist needs to set up basic information such as checkout limits, the amount of time a book can be checked out, and other basic housekeeping information.

The conversion to an automated system is a lot of work, but the benefits far outweigh the time it takes to complete the process.

Skill 18.3   Identify purposes and procedures for conducting a library media collection inventory

Conducting inventory is the process of verifying the collection holdings and assessing the collection's physical condition. Its purposes including the following:

1.   To indicate lost or missing materials and identify items for replacement.
2.   To reveal strengths and weaknesses in collection, helping identify areas where numbers of materials do not reflect need.
3.   To identify materials needing repair. Periodic preventive maintenance can save major repair or replacement cost.
4.   To shape the process of weeding. Outdated and damaged or worn materials would be removed to maintain the integrity of the collection's reputation.

Procedures:

1.   Specify when inventory will be conducted. Most schools conduct inventories at the end of the school year. Many districts require inventory statistics be turned into the school or district supervisors before media staff vacations.

2.   Determine who will conduct inventory. Personnel availability will determine whether inventory will be conducted by professionals, support staff, or some combination of the two during school hours or during closed time.

3.   Examine each item and match it to the holding records, pulling items that need repair.

4.   Tabulate results and record on forms required by the school or district.

Skill 18.4   Identify procedures for maintaining a current collection relevant to the school's instructional program

A collection of resources that closely ties the school's instructional program as well as the developmental and cultural needs of students is crucial to the school library media program.

To ensure the collection meets student needs there are steps the media specialist can take:

1.   Stay abreast of changes in curriculum as well as the types of resources needed to meet those needs.

2.   Work closely with teachers to determine resources needed.

3.   Work closely with staff to determine policies and procedures.

4.   Develop specific processes for evaluating and updating the collection.

5.   Have access to up-to-date collection monitoring and evaluation tools and reviewing resources.

6.   Support the circulation of resources by sharing information with teachers and allowing them to preview new resources as well as take part in the selection process.

Skill 18.5   Identify the criteria for weeding a collection

There are many resources that provide assistance with weeding procedures. When reviewing a collection for weeding, a media specialist should consider that weeding is an ongoing process. Oftentimes, weeding is a subjective process; thus, the media specialist should also base the activity on the following categories:

USE – Look for materials not circulated regularly

WEAR – torn, stained, or ripped materials may need to be repaired or let go

SUBJECT – the information in the resource is outdated or no longer valid or has been replaced by a newer, updated version of the material

AVAILABLE ELSEWHERE – if the material is readily available electronically or through another resource and is not often used, it may be worth discarding

When weeding, consider extenuating circumstances that might warrant the saving of materials, such as works by local authors, memorial gifts or local histories.

Here are the suggested weeding procedures for each Dewey level:

- 000 – encyclopedias every five years, other materials no more than eight years
- 100 – five to eight years
- 200 – can be high turnover with religious books – keep current
- 300 – replace almanacs every two years and keep political information current
- 400 – check for wear and tear frequently
- 500 – continuously update to make sure scientific information is current
- 600 – continuously update medical information as older information can be misleading or dangerous
- 700 – keep until worn
- 800 – keep until worn
- 900 – weed about every two years
- Biography – keep most current or best written titles
- Adult fiction – weed for multiple copies, keeping those in best shape and that have the most literary value
- Young-adult and children's fiction – same as adult fiction
- Reference – weed for currency and accuracy

COMPETENCY 19.0   COMPREHENSION OF LEADERSHIP AND INTERPERSONAL SKILLS FOR THE LIBRARY MEDIA SPECIALIST

Skill 19.1   Identify ways to promote collaborative relationships among the library media staff and school staff, students and community members

The school library media specialist must establish rapport with all groups in the school community. To promote this collaboration, he or she should involve representatives from these groups in the development, implementation, and evaluation of the school library media program. To increase the involvement of school community members, follow these tactics:

1.   Establish a library media advisory committee.
2.   Solicit expert advice from teachers on selecting and weeding collection materials.
3.   Promote the program and solicit suggestions for improvement.
4.   Establish a reciprocal working relationship with the school principal and/or supervisor of media.
5.   Conduct workshops or lessons on using the media center as a resource center.

These activities will immerse the school community in the library media program, building the rapport of both the specialist and the program and increasing collaboration from all levels of school leadership.

Skill 19.2   Identify leadership opportunities and techniques for a library media specialist's involvement in the school program

A good leader should be able to work and inspire others to work in a team environment where the input of team members at all levels is encouraged and appreciated. When a library media specialist undertakes a leadership role, he or she enhances the collaborative nature of the entire learning community. To accomplish this goal, a good leader should:

1.   Exhibit the desire to achieve the goals of an efficient library media program.
2.   Show appreciation for the contributions of library media staff and supervise them in a democratic style.
3.   Delegate tasks to responsible staff members.
4.   Engage in continuing education.
5.   Maintain active membership in professional organizations.
6.   Show respect and concern for colleagues and superiors.

Skill 19.3 **Identify interpersonal skills that can produce positive collaborative relationships**

One of the single most important parts of a successful school library media program is collaboration between the school library media specialist and classroom teachers. Oftentimes, this collaboration is enhanced with strong interpersonal relationships. In order to develop such a connection in a learning community, a library media specialist must possess key interpersonal skills in the work environment. These include:

- **Flexibility** to adjust to the differing logistical and scheduling needs of staff and students.
- **Expertise** in the curriculum being taught at the grade levels being served. This makes the media specialist and invaluable collaborative partner.
- **Leadership** to set the goals for and expectations of the media program should move towards. Strong leadership skills will also help the specialist be the advocate for the teachers as well as the media program.
- **Approachability** to establish good rapport with staff and students. The specialist should establish a reputation of being one who takes the extra step for teachers and students.
- **Persistence** to keep going and keep the media program moving forward.

COMPETENCY 20.0   KNOWLEDGE OF STATE AND NATIONAL LEGISLATION AND ITS EFFECTS

Skill 20.1   Identify specific state legislation and its effect on library media programs

Because regulations and standards are in place at the local, district, state, regional, and national levels, a library media specialist must be aware of key legislation and decision making that affects library media program. Here are several examples that the library media specialist should be aware of when working in the state of Florida:

1986 State of Florida created a special appropriation of 17 million dollars in matching funds for upgrading and expanding library media materials and equipment in public schools.

1990 State of Florida provided funding for SUNLINK, the DOE Division of

School Library Media Services for retrospective conversion of public school libraries to create statewide interlibrary loan network (funding continued through 1996-97).

1991 Blueprint 2000, a System of School Improvement and Accountability.

This legislation transfers authority for the design of effective programs to local control and mandates formation of school improvement plans to hold schools accountable for performance of students. Though library media programs are not specifically mentioned in the Blueprint 2000 goals, Goal 4 charges schools with the provision of a conducive learning environment, a goal enhanced by a successful library media program.

1993 Florida State Statutes address library media as follows:

231.15 specifies that like other certification areas (e.g., teacher, guidance counselor, principal, and athletic coach), a school library media specialist must meet the law requiring certification in his or her content area (1.7).

233.165 specifies that selection of instructional materials, library books, and other material used in the public schools shall meet the standards of materials propriety.

1.   The age of the children who normally would be expected to have access to the materials
2.   The educational purpose to be served by the material
3.   The degree of mature classroom discussion of the material

4.   The consideration of the broad socioeconomic, ethnic, racial, and cultural diversity of the children

This article also prohibits the procurement of material with hard-core pornography.

233.34 deals with funding for instructional materials, specifies that library and reference books may be purchased from the 50% of the instructional materials allocation that need not be ordered from the state adopted list.

Skill 20.2   Identify specific national legislation and its effect on library media programs

1965   Elementary and Secondary Education Act Title III

This legislation impacted school libraries by encouraging their expansion into media centers.

1981   Education Consolidation and Improvement Act

Chapter II of this bill included regulations and funding in the form of block grants for school library media resources and instructional equipment. Funding ended with the 1994-95 school year.

1995   Innovative Educational Programs Legislation

This three-year program provided block grants for innovative uses of technology in schools, including library media centers.

2001   Child Internet Protection Act

This imposes specific requirements on any school or library that receives funding support for Internet access or internal connections from the "E-rate" program.

2001   USA PATRIOT Act

This act was created to update wiretap and surveillance laws for the Internet age. Its focus was to address various types of communications (e.g., email and voice mail) and to give law enforcement greater authority to conduct property searches.

COMPETENCY 21.0 KNOWLEDGE OF THE HISTORICAL DEVELOPMENT OF SCHOOL LIBRARY MEDIA PROGRAMS

Skill 21.1 Identify the areas in which technology has changed school library media programs

Technology has created the engines of access and also contributed to the volume of available information. In addition to learning the types of equipment, their functions, and methods for demonstrating their uses to teachers and students, the school library media specialist must also locate or design lessons that will teach the 'search and sift' techniques that help them find the appropriate information for a given need. Critical evaluation of the reading and application of the new information to previous knowledge are skills that must be accomplished.

Many school library media specialists have accepted the title without making the adaptation. They feel overloaded by the magnitude of the job description and connect contextualize new advances in technology and how these advances build upon a user's knowledge base. Oftentimes, districts approach technology enhancement by putting the hardware before the program.

Just placing computers, CD players, audio equipment, video cameras, software and so many other types of equipment in the schools achieves nothing in regard to benefiting the learners, especially if the equipment gathers dust. Program development is often an afterthought, from necessity.

Program development should, in fact, precede the acquisition of new technologies. After all, societal changes have had profound effects on schools. Ethnic diversity, non-traditional families, poverty, and population mobility have created social and cultural problems that did not exist thirty years ago. Furthermore, children raised in this ever-shifting social network must be prepared with skills that will enable them to become productive, literate adults. Library media centers are charged with the responsibility of motivating interest in reading as well as promoting acquisition of skills, of providing reading that will not only inform but help children learn how to cope with and enjoy life. Thus, the library media specialist needs to pay attention to how programming fits into the technological advances of society in coordination with the equipment available in the media center.

Since technology increases the volume of all types of information, issues regarding censorship and intellectual access increase, as well. Media professionals must learn how to handle challenges to the material in and accessible from their media centers, and they must guard their patrons' right to free access. Interpreting fair use and other copyright issues requires constant monitoring of court cases and changes in the law. The impact of all of these issues has and will continue to affect school library media programs.

Skill 21.2   Identify the effects of societal changes on school library media programs

Until the passage of the Elementary and Secondary Education Act in 1965, which encouraged the evolution of school libraries into library media centers, school libraries were deemed repositories of print material, mainly reference books and works of fiction. School librarians, rarely having a support staff, managed circulated and processed materials, supervised student behavior in the library, maintained the collection, and distributed limited equipment. The explosion of information and the retrieval systems for accessing that information has revolutionized the role of the school library media specialist and the program he or she oversees, as library media programs are now undertaking responsibility for acquainting students with societal advances in technology.

Societal changes have long held influence over school library media programs. In post-World War II America, studies in child development by Jean Piaget, Erik Erikson and Lawrence Kohlberg began to affect collection development. Learning style theories from Abraham Maslow's hierarchy to Howard Gardner's eight intelligences have modified classroom teaching, and in turn, the collections necessary to create a successful learning environment.

In the 1980's legislative actions at the national and state level, government concern for widespread literacy, and document findings such as those in *A Nation at Risk* have all reinforced that instruction must be improved in all areas. As a result of private publications such as James Naisbitt's *Megatrends* and *Megatrends 2000* and research by the staff of *School Library Media Quarterly*, the issue of providing more than mere access to the wealth of information affects libraries in the public and private sector. Ultimately, the school library media specialist becomes the agent through which the most aggressive change will occur.

In 1983, Dr. Shirley Aaron, a professor of library science at Florida State University, and Pat Scales, a school library media specialist at Greenville Middle School in South Carolina, undertook a significant project: to produce an annual report. Each volume has sections of articles on issues of current interest, legislation, professional organizations' reports, trends, and forecasts. By 1988, Jane B. Smith, school library media consultant to the Alabama Department of Education, assumed the role of managing editor. Author of several books herself, Ms. Smith has become one of the experts in school library media. Dr. Phyllis Van Orden, also an FSU professor in the Division of Library and Information Management, has authored a major book on collection development. In 1988, *Information Power* was published under the supervision of AASL president, Karen Whitney, and AECT president, Elaine Didier. In the same year *Taxonomies of the School Library Media Program* by David Loertscher, senior acquisitions editor for Libraries Unlimited, appeared. In fact, there is now a considerable body of excellent reference material on school library media.

As libraries began to evolve into full service media centers and school media specialists became instructional consultants to teachers, all aspects of program development were influenced by the need to know the factors that influence children's learning. The ability to assess the needs of student users of a particular media center's services and resources has become a collaborative effort with the classroom teachers who have daily contact with their students; thus, the 1990's moved education towards cooperative planning and cooperative learning.

COMPETENCY 22.0   KNOWLEDGE OF PROFESSIONAL ORGANIZATIONS AND RESOURCES

Skill 22.1   Identify state and national library media professional associations

<u>Library Media Organizations</u>

National:

American Association of School Library (AASL)
American Library Association
50 East Huron Street
Chicago IL 60611

Association for Educational Communications and Technology (AECT)
1126 Sixteenth Street, NW
Washington DC 20036

State:

Florida Association for Media in Education (FAME)
P. O. Box 13119
Tallahassee FL 32308

Local:

Local affiliates of state organizations such as FAME

Public library support groups

<u>Related Organizations</u>

National:

National Education Association (NEA)
1201 North Street NW
Washington DC 20036-3290

American Federation of Teachers (AFT)
555 New Jersey Avenue, NW
Washington DC 20001-2079

Phi Delta Kappa International, Inc.
408 N. Union
P. O. Box 789
Bloomington IN 47402

International Reading Association
800 Barksdale Road
Newark DE 19711-3269

Association of Supervision and Curriculum Development (ASCD)
1250 N. Pitt Street
Alexandria VA 22314-1453

State and Local:

State and local affiliates of NEA

State and local affiliates of AFT

Skill 22.2 Identify the major concepts in the national school library media guidelines

Information Power: Building Partnerships for Learning provides a detailed road map for school library media specialists to follow. The major concepts outlined in this publication include:

- providing access to resources and information through integrated activities on a variety of levels
- providing physical access to a wide variety of resources and information from various locations including outside agencies and electronic resources
- assisting patrons in locating and evaluating information
- collaborating with teachers and others
- facilitating the lifelong learning process
- building a school library media program that acts as the hub of all learning within the school
- providing resources that embrace differences culturally and socially and support concepts of intellectual freedom

Skill 22.3   Identify library media professional development resources and their space

As evidenced by the resource list in this guide, professional development resources are extensive in scope.

Other sources include the college and university programs offered at many state and private institutions. Degrees in library science, information science, or educational media are offered for both undergraduates and graduate students. Some universities also offer extern programs or on-line courses.

Workshops are offered at state conferences and through district inservice programs.

State Certification requirements adopted in 1992 offer two plans to prepare individuals for becoming a media services professional:

1.   A bachelor's or higher degree with an undergraduate or graduate major in educational media.

2.   A bachelor's or higher degree with thirty (30) semester hours in educational media.

The list of resources at the end of this guide detail many titles which provide information on school library media programs. *Information Power* (AASL/AECT), *Taxonomies of the School Library Media Program* (Loertscher), and *Administering the School Library Media Center* (Gillespie and Spirt) are three of the best-known and most accessible.

While less accessible but still a valuable reference tool, the six volume set titled *School Library Media Annual* (Smith, Aaron, and Scales, Eds.) deals with different aspects of school library media programs.

The Florida DOE's *Florida School Library Media Programs: A Guide for Excellence*, though twenty years old, also provides sound guidelines for media programs that are still relevant to today's library media specialist. Many of the recommendations are only now being implemented in some schools.

Among periodicals, *The School Library Media Quarterly* (AASL) offers scholarly articles that are research based. *The Florida Media Quarterly*, a publication of the Florida Association for Media in Education, offers many excellent articles written by Florida educators, and each issue has a concise legislative review. *Media and Methods* presents information on integrating media into curriculum. *Tech Trends* (AECT) also examines the impact of technology and innovations in media use.

COMPETENCY 23.0 KNOWLEDGE OF CURRENT PROFESSIONAL TRENDS AND ISSUES

Skill 23.1 Identify the principles of intellectual freedom

The principles of intellectual freedom are guaranteed by the First Amendment to the Constitution of the United States. They are reinforced in the Library Bill of Rights adapted by the ALA in 1948, the AECT's statement on intellectual freedom (1978), the freedom to read and review statements of the ALA (1953 and 1979), and the National Council of English Teachers in its Students' Right to Read Statement.

These principles, as they relate to children, include the following:

1.   Freedom of access to information in all formats through activities that develop critical thinking and problem solving skills.
2.   Freedom of access to ideas that present a variety of points of view through activities with goals to teach discriminating reading.
3.   Freedom to acquire information reflective of the intellectual, physical, and social growth of the user.

It becomes the responsibility of the school library media specialist to develop and maintain collection development and distribution policies that ensures these freedoms.

Skill 23.2 Identify the impact of court cases pertaining to copyright and First Amendment rights

Judicial rulings have come in the area of copyright issues, and a media specialist should be aware of these as he or she works with teachers and students to acquire and use information. The 1975 ruling in the case of *Williams & Wilkins Co. v. U.S.* provided guidance to legislators in preparing the fair use provisions of the 1976 Copyright Act.

It ruled that entire articles may be mass-duplicated for use which advances the public welfare without doing economic harm to the publishers. This ruling provides encouragement to educators, as fair use can be interpreted more liberally.

In 1984, the ruling in the *Sony Corp. of America v. Universal City Studios, Inc.* placed the burden of proving infringement on the plaintiff. The Supreme Court upheld the right of individuals to off-air videotape television programs for non-commercial use. Thus, a copyright holder must prove that the use of videotaped programming is intentionally harmful. Civil suits against educators would require the plaintiff to prove that the existing or potential market would be negatively affected by use of these programs in a classroom setting. Current fair use practice specifies that a videotaped copy must be shown within 10 days of its airing and be kept no longer than 45 days for use in constructing supplemental teaching materials related to the programming.

Court rulings have ambiguously addressed the issue of censorship and written texts. In 1972, the U.S. Court of Appeals for the Second Circuit (*President's Council v. Community School Board No. 25, New York City*) ruled in favor of the removal of a library book, reasoning that its removal did not oppose or aid religion.

In 1976, the Court of Appeals for the Sixth Circuit (*Minarcini v. Strongsville City School District*) ruled against the removal of Joseph Heller's *Catch 22* and two Kurt Vonnegut novels on the grounds that removal of books from a school library is a burden on the freedom of classroom discussion and an infringement of the First Amendment's guarantee of an individual's "right to know."

A Massachusetts district court (*Right to Read Defense Committee v. School Board of the City of Chelsea*) ordered the school board to return a poetry anthology which contained "objectionable and filthy" language to the high school library. The court asserted that the school had control over curriculum but not library collections.

Three cases in the 1980's also dealt with challenging the removal of materials from high school libraries. The first two, in circuit courts, condemned the burning of banned books (*Zykan v. Warsaw Community School Corporation, Indiana*) and the removal of books of considerable literary merit. The case of *Board of Education, Island Trees Union Free School District 26 (New York) v. Pico* reached the Supreme Court in 1982 after the U.S. Court of Appeals for the Second Circuit had reversed a lower court ruling granting the school board the right to remove nine books which had been deemed "anti-American, anti-Semitic, anti-Christian and just plain filthy." In a 5-4 ruling, the Supreme Court upheld the Court of Appeals' ruling and the nine books were returned. The dissenting opinion, however, continued to foster ambiguity, claiming that if the intent was to deny free access to ideas, it was an infringement of the First Amendment, but if the intent was to remove pervasively vulgar material, the board had just cause. Ultimately, the issue hinged on a school board's authority in determining the selection of optional rather than required reading. Library books, being optional, should not be denied to users.

Skill 23.3   Identify the implications of flexible access

The issue of flexible access is especially distressing to elementary school library media specialists who are placed in the "related arts wheel," providing planning time for art, music, and physical education teachers. "Closed" or rigid scheduling (i.e., scheduling classes to meet regularly for instruction in the library) prohibits the implementation of the integrated program philosophy essential to the principles of intellectual freedom.

The AASL Position Statement on Flexible Scheduling asserts that schools must adopt a philosophy of full integration of library media into the total educational program. This integration assures a partnership of students, teachers, and school library media specialists in the use of readily accessible materials and services when they are appropriate to the classroom curriculum

All parties in the school community, including teachers, principal, district administration, and the school board, must share the responsibility for contributing to flexible access.

Research on the validity of flexible access reinforces the need for cooperative planning with teachers, an objective that cannot be met if the school library media specialist has no time for the required planning sessions. Rigid scheduling denies students the freedom to come to the library during the school day for pleasurable reading and self-motivated inquiry activities vital to the development of critical thinking, problem solving, and exploratory skills. Without flexible access, the library becomes just another self-contained classroom.

Skill 23.4   Identify the implications of shared resources on library media programs

Resource sharing has always been an integral part of education. Before the technology revolution, sharing was done within schools or departments and between teachers. Now, members of the school community have the potential to access information from around the world.

Resource sharing is a way of

1.   Providing a broader information base to enable users to find and access the resources that provide the needed information.
2.   Reducing or containing media center budgets.
3.   Establishing cooperation with other resource providers that encourage mutual planning and standardization of control.

Resource sharing systems include:

1. **Interlibrary loan**. The advent of computer databases has simplified the process of locating sources in other libraries. Local public library collections can be accessed from terminals in the media center. Physical access depends on going to the branch where the material is housed.

2. **Networking systems**. Sharing information has become even easier with the use of network services. Files can be shared and accessed from room to room, school to school and city to city. Resources can be shared within a small geographic location such as a school by the use of a local area network, or LAN. A wide area network, or WAN, is used to communicate over a larger area such as a school district or city.
    a. E-mail allows educators to communicate across the state.
    b. On-line services (i.e., Internet providers) offer access to a specific menu of locations. Monthly fees and time charges must be budgeted.
    c. Individual city or county network systems. These are community sponsored networks, often part of the public library system, which provide Internet access for the price of a local phone call. A time limit usually confines an individual search to allow more users access.
    d. On-line continuing education programs offer courses and degrees through at-home study. Large school districts provide lessons for homebound students or home school advocates.
    e. Bulletin boards allow individuals or groups to converse electronically with persons in another place.

3. **Telecommunications**. Using telephone and television as the media for communication, telecommunications is used primarily for distance learning. Many universities or networks of universities provide workshops, conferences and college credit courses for educators. They also offer courses for senior high school students in subjects that could not generate adequate class counts in their home schools. Large school districts offer broadcast programming for homebound or home schooled students. The advantage of telecommunication programming (as opposed to networking systems) is that students are provided with a phone number so they can interact with the instructors or information providers.

Skill 23.5   Identify the challenges to the library media specialist created by the new technologies

School library media specialists have always been responsible for instructing students and teachers in the use of equipment and the media used with them.

Now they must also teach both teachers and students how to use computers and their applications. If the media center has only computers for the automated catalog, the instruction is usually done for individuals or small groups as they need to locate materials. Peer instruction can be very efficient in using automated indexes. Student library aides or volunteers can also assist with informal instruction.

If the media center has an attached computer lab, operation of and instruction in the lab may also become the specialist's responsibility. Support staff or paraprofessionals can supervise laboratory activities, and the classroom teacher can provide content instruction and/or operational procedure.

In addition, the media specialist is often expected to be the technician responsible for cleaning and maintaining the technologies in the media center and throughout the school. In small districts, technical assistance may be provided by the district computer department, through an external contractor, or by the technical division of the company from whom the technology has been provided.

As more technologies are integrated into the school environment, the media specialist must clarify expectations for maintenance, instruction, and supervision, altering budgetary needs as he or she sees fit.

COMPETENCY 24.0   KNOWLEDGE OF RESEARCH

Skill 24.1   Identify information sources that document research pertaining to school library media programs

One of the most abundant resources for research on libraries would be the American Library Association's website and publications where there is a wealth of information covering topics from collection development to advocacy.

As a subsidiary of ALA, the American Association of School Librarians focuses specifically on the needs of school libraries. The have published a wide array of resources to make a school library media program more effective. One such resource is their research journal, *School Library Media Research,* which spotlights the latest trends. Another publication from AASL is *Knowledge Quest* and its online companion, *KQWeb.* Both focus on the integration of latest trends.

SUNLINK provides information pertinent to media specialists operating in Florida. Developed by the Florida Department of Education, this guide is specifically produced for school library media specialists.

The Library Power Executive Summary also serves as a great resource for library media professionals, as it outlines the information derived from one of the largest research efforts covering library media programs.

Skill 24.2   Evaluate research data

Since research information can have a profound effect on the goals of a library media program, a specialist should evaluate research data in order to see whether it pertains to the needs and direction of his or her particular program. When reviewing research information, there are key questions to consider:

1.   What was the topic of the report?
2.   How does the information found in this project fit what is known?
3.   How was the research completed?
4.   What were the outcomes of the study?
5.   What can be determined from the study results?

Skill 24.3 Identify ways research can be used to validate school library media programs

The use of research to validate school library media programs can be beneficial in many ways:

1. Information found in research can serve as a guide for planning the direction of the program.
2. The information can serve as a baseline from which individual programs can be measured.
3. It can provide support for future initiatives and budget requests.

A media specialist should use significant research to promote the continual development of the library media program. Not only can such research help in the selection of collection materials, but the research can also be used to reinforce the importance of integrating the library media program throughout a school's curriculum. A library media specialist should cull and summarize important research and present his or her findings at appropriate planning and committee meetings.

COMPETENCY 25.0   KNOWLEDGE OF PROFESSIONAL ETHICS

Skill 25.1   Identify an ethical course of action for a copyright issue

When a suspected infringement of copyright is brought to the attention of the school library media specialist, he or she should follow certain procedures.

1.   Determine if a violation has in effect occurred. Never accuse or report alleged instances to a higher authority without verification.

2.   If an instance is verified, tactfully inform the violator of the specific criteria to use so that future violations can be avoided. Presented properly, the information will be accepted as constructive.

3.   If advice is unheeded and further infractions occur, bring them to the attention of the teacher's supervisor (i.e., a team leader or department chair) who can handle the matter as an evaluation procedure.

4.   Inform the person who has reported the alleged violation of the procedures being used.

Oftentimes, infringement of copyright is based on poor communication between the media specialist and the violator. First and foremost, the media specialist should be proactive in establishing accepted policies for copyright and fair use, and he or she should also remind a community member of these policies when he or she infracts upon the rules.

Skill 25.2   Identify an ethical course of action for an intellectual freedom issue

Despite the best collection development policies, an occasional complaint concerning intellectual freedom will arise. In our society the following issues cause controversy: politics, gay rights, profanity, pornography, creationism vs. evolution, the occult, sex education, racism, and violence. Adults disagree philosophically about these issues. They will often express their concern first to the school library media specialist.

Ethically, the specialist is bound to protect the principles of intellectual freedom, but he or she is also bound by those same principles to treat the complaint seriously as the expression of an opposing view. When a complaint comes before a media specialist, he or she should not panic. The challenge is not an affront to the media specialist but a complaint about the content, language, or graphics in a material.

The first step is to greet the complainant calmly and explain the principles of intellectual freedom a specialist is bound to uphold. A good paraphrase from the AECT Statement is that a learner's right to access information can only be abridged by an agreement between parent and child. This can easily be related by discussing the current emphasis on the V chip for selective television viewing. With the V Chip, parents are becoming more aware of their own roles in censoring unwanted images from their children. Parents must take an active role of mediating information for their children and cannot rely on providers to do the work for them.

In most instances, a calm, rational discussion will satisfy the challenger. However, if the challenge is pursued, the media specialist will have to follow district procedures for handling the complaint. The appropriate school administrator should be informed, even if an administrator handled the initial confrontation. The complainant should be asked to fill out a formal complaint form, citing his or her specific objection in a logical manner. Sometimes, simply thinking the issue through clearly and recognizing that someone will truly listen to his or her complaint is enough of a solution. If all else fails, a reconsideration committee should be appointed to take the matter under advisement and recommend a course of action.

Skill 25.3   Identify an ethical course of action for a confidentiality issue

At some point in his or her career, a specialist may be asked to account for a community member's activities within the library media center. Such action has come to the forefront given the changes in policy as outlined in the US PATRIOT Act. Suggested procedures include the following:

1. When a request is made, explain the confidentiality policy.
2. Consult with the appropriate legal authority to determine if such process, order, or subpoena is in good form and if there is a just cause for its issuance.
3. If the process is not in proper form or if just cause has not been shown, the library should insist that this be remedied before any records are released.
4. Generally a subpoena *duces tecum* (i.e., bring your records) requires the responsible library officer to attend court or to provide testimony at his or her deposition. It also may require that certain circulation records be submitted.
5. Staff should be trained and required to report any threats not supported by a process, order, or subpoena concerning the records.
6. If any problems arise, refer the requestor to the responsible legal council.

RESOURCES

1.   American Association of School Librarians and Association for Educational Communications and Technology. *Information Power: Guidelines for School Library Media Programs.* Chicago: American Library Association and Association for Educational Communications and Technology, 1988.

     A sourcebook for presenting professional guidelines for developing school library media programs for the 1990's and into the twentieth century. It includes chapters on establishing and maintaining a school library media program; defining the role of the school library media professional and paraprofessional personnel; determining the resources, equipment, and facilities necessary to meet the goals; and spelling out leadership responsibilities of the district, region, and state. Appendices contain policy statements from different organizations, present research results, and provide budget formulas and minimum standards for facilities spaces.

2.   American Association of School Librarians and Association for Educational Communication and Technology. *Information Power: Building Partnerships for Learning.* Chicago: American Library Association and Association for Educational Communications and Technology, 1998.

     A follow-up to the publication *Information Power: Guidelines for School Library Media Programs.* It includes chapters on information literacy, collaboration, learning and teaching, information access, program administration, and connecting with the learning community. The appendices contain information on various statements and policies from various organizations.

3.   American Library Association, Canadian Library Association, and The Library Association. *Anglo-American Cataloging Rules.* 2nd ed. Chicago: American Library Association, 1988.

     A revised edition which provides rules for including technology changes.

4.   American Library Association, Office for Intellectual Freedom Staff. *Intellectual Freedom Manual* . 2nd ed. Chicago: American Library Association, 1983.

    Updated in 1998, this manual presents the statements of rights of various library organizations, provides the ALA Intellectual Freedom statement and its implications for library media programs, discusses laws and court cases, advises on methods to deal with censorship, and presents promotion techniques.

5.   Anderson, Pauline H. *Planning School Library Media Facilities*. Hamden, CT: The Shoe String Press, Inc., 1990.

    This extensive work traces the creation of a school library media center from politicking to moving in. Much emphasis is placed on the planning process. Five specific case studies are offered to show how the process works.

6.   Baker, Philip D. *The Library Media Center and the School*. Littleton, CO: Libraries Unlimited, 1984.

    A thorough discussion of the school library media program in relation to the total school mission and objectives.

7.   Bannister, Barbara Farley and Janice B. Carlile. *Elementary School Librarian's Survival Guide*. New York: The Center for Applied Research in Education, 1993.

    A great guide for either setting up a new media center or operating an existing one. It deals with the physical management of the media center; successful discipline; reading promotions; special programs; story times, book talks, and library skills; building support with the school community; budgeting; selection procedures; new technologies; inventory and weeding; and avoiding burnout. Full of practical suggestions and reproducibles.

8.   Brown, J. W.; R.B. Lewis; and F. F. Harcleroad. *A V Introduction: Technology, Media, and Methods*. 6th ed. New York: McGraw-Hill, 1983.

    A good reference book on the use of instructional materials and technology at all educational levels. It provides information on planning instruction, using and producing various media, operating audio-visual equipment, and designing facilities for using media. It also provides information on copyright laws.

9.   Buchanan, Jan. *Flexible Access Media Programs.* Littleton, CO: Libraries Unlimited, 1991.

A fine reference tool for understanding and developing approaches to designing flexible access programs for school library media centers. It presents an overview of current research on integrating the teaching of library skills into the curriculum, a whole language approach to reading instruction, and the importance of encouraging critical thinking. The book's greatest value is showing the building level media specialist the techniques for involving the entire school community in the planning and implementation of integrated lessons and defining the roles of all the participants involved in the planning, execution and evaluation stages. Emphasis is on the cooperative planning required and on the measurable benefit to the learner.

10.   Bucher, Katherine Toth. *Computers & Technology in School Library Media Centers.* Worthington, OH: Linworth Publishing, Inc., 1994.

This 3-ring bound publication offers a thorough discussion of technology's relevance to libraries. It includes as contents (1) working with instructional technology in the 1990's, (2) computer basics, (3) library management with a computer, (4) multimedia CD-ROM, and (5) videodisks in the library.

11.   Carlsen, G. Robert. *Books and the Teenage Reader.* New York: Harper and Row, 1971.

This ageless work discusses teenage interests and social/personal needs and provides reading lists in different genres, interest areas, and the classics.

12.   Curley, Arthur. "Yes for ALA Goal 2000." *Florida Media Quarterly* 1995: Volume 20, Number 3: 24.

A short article specifying the Goal 2000 theme and the value of its message for school library media programs.

13.   Donelson, K. L. and A. P. Nilsen. *Literature for Today's Young Adults.* 3rd ed. Glenview, IL: Scott, Foresman, 1989.

A textbook dealing with print media: the history and trends of young adult literature; genres of special interest; using materials with young adults; and guidelines for evaluating these works. Presents brief statements about works of both recognized merit and potential interest to young adults while also providing biographical sketches of authors known in the field.

14. Downing, Mildred Harlow and David H. Downing. *Introduction to Cataloging and Classification.* 6th ed. Jefferson, NC: McFarland & Company, Inc., 1992.

A basic primer on cataloguing techniques and classification systems.

15. Florida Department of Education, Division of Public Schools, Bureau of Program Support Services, School Library Media Services Section. *Information Skills for Florida Schools K-12* Tallahassee, FL: Florida Department of Education, 1984.

A concise scope and sequence for the teaching of library skills. Offers a fold-out chart for readily identifying skills at their introductory, review, reinforcement, and expansion stages.

16. Florida Department of Education, School Library Media Services Section. *Florida School Library Media Programs: A Guide for Excellence.* Tallahassee, FL: Florida Department of Education, 1976.

State guidelines, developed from the 1975 AASL-AECT *Media Programs: District and School*, establishing criteria for local, district, and state media services. It provides details for school level media personnel regarding the program responsibilities, operational procedures, personnel duties, resource development, and facilities.

17. Florida Division of Statutory Revision of the Joint Legislative Management Committee. *Official Florida Statutes, 1993.* Tallahassee, FL: State of Florida.

Biennial set of complete laws governing the state, published in odd numbered years. Supplements printed in even numbered years.

18. Gillespie, J. T. (Ed.) *Best Books for Junior High Readers.* New Providence, NJ: Bowker, 1991.

A reference guide to selecting titles for junior high (upper middle school) readers. Presents examples of literature within certain genres, discusses themes appropriate to middle grade readers based on personal, social, and academic needs.

19.   Gillespie, J. T. and L. Spirt. *Administering the School Library Media Center*. New York: Bowker, 1983.

      A guide to practical considerations in operating a school library media center. Chapters on acquisition, organization, and management, with chapters on new technologies. Presents example of a policies and procedures manual. Revised in 1993.

20.   Hagler, Ronald. *The Bibliographic Record and Information Technology*. 2nd ed. Chicago, IL: American Library Association, 1991.

      A serious, detailed study of cataloging, bibliographic standards and controls using MARC record format.

21.   Hannigan, J.a. and Glenn Estes. *Media Center Facilities Design*. Chicago, IL: American Library Association, 1978.

      Expanding on the ALA discussion of facilities design in *Information Power,* these authors have presented methods and models for media facilities for all school levels, discussing factors for planning, design, and construction even offering architectural renderings.

22.   Hart, Thomas. *Behavior Management in the School Library Media Center*. Chicago, IL: American Library Association, 1985.

      A serious work on the positive educational strategies for managing student behavior in the use the resources and services of the school library media center.

23.   Haycock, Ken. "Research in Teacher-Librarianship and the Institutionalization of Change." *School Library Media Quarterly* (Summer 1995): 227-233.

      This paper contends that there is ample research to prove the relationship between student achievement and the instructional role of library media specialist. Mr. Haycock offers this evidence and a 92-item annotation to point out the strong statistical support that can be used to promote programs.

24. *The School Library Program in the Curriculum.* Englewood CO: Libraries Unlimited, Inc., 1990.

     This collection of essays and opinion papers by Haycock and others deals with the media center in the context of the total school, the role of the teacher librarian, the facets of program planning and development, the task of integrating information skills across the curriculum, applications in secondary school, and issues and concerns.

25. Heinrich, R.; M. Molenda; and J.D. Russell. *Instructional Media and the New Technologies of Instruction.* 2nd ed. New York: Macmillan, 1985.

     A textbook source for planning and using of non-print media. Full of charts, diagrams, and appendices on sources for free and inexpensive materials.

26. Helm, V. M. *What Educators Should Know About Copyright.* Phi Delta Kappa Educational Foundation, 1986.

     A brief, but thorough discussion of copyright law, the court cases that have tested that law, and the implications of the rulings on schools, including library media programs.

27. Huck, C. S.; S. Hepler; and J. Hickman. *Children's Literature in the Elementary School.* 4th ed. New York: Holt, Rhinehart and Winston, 1987.

     Both a textbook in child development and the literature designed to meet children's needs. Provides a study of genres and a presentation of methods for teaching children's literature. Lists of book awards, authors, illustrators, periodicals and publishers.

28. Inter, Sheila S. *Circulation Policy in Academic, Public, and School Libraries.* New York: Greenwood Press, 1987.

     This book deals with circulation policies in academic, public, and school libraries. Specific circulation plans from schools around the country offer models.

29. Inter, Sheila S. and Jean Weichs. *Standard Cataloguing for School and Public Libraries.* Englewood, CO: Libraries Unlimited, 1990.

Written for public librarians and school library media specialists, this book explains the principles and standards of cataloging. Though a thorough discussion of AACR rules, descriptions, subject headings, classification systems, the book avoids discussing arcane details that are most likely not encountered by the intended audience.

30. Katz, W.a. *Introduction to Reference Work.* (Vol. 1) Basic Information Sources. 5th ed. New York: McGraw Hill, 1987.

A study of traditional basic reference sources and methods for using these sources to answer reference questions. Includes an overview of the reference process and on-line reference services and their applications.

31. Kemp, J. E. *Planning and Producing Audio-visual Materials.* 4th ed. New York: Harper & Row, 1980.

Practical guide to media production techniques and methods of instruction. Summarizes research on the effectiveness of instructional materials and explains the method of developing an instructional program.

32. Kinney, Lisa F. *Lobby for Your Library-Know What Works.* Chicago, IL: American Library Association, 1992.

Chapter 8 deals specifically with lobbying for schools, presenting typical funding sources and offering strategies to be used by key participants in lobbying agencies from local to state.

33. Klasing, Jane P. *Designing and Renovating School Library Media Centers.* Chicago, IL: American Library Association, 1991.

A quick reference for use by school personnel in planning and implementing an efficient facilities design. Sample floor plans and appendices full of bid forms, architectural symbols, and furniture details simplify the process.

34. Lance, Keith Curry. *The Impact of School Library Media Centers on Academic Achievement*. Castle Rock, CO: Willow Research and Publishing, 1993.

Predominantly a research-based discussion of factors of library media programs that have directly influenced the improvement in student grades, standardized scores, and self-directed learning.

35. Laughlin, Mildred Knight and Kathy Howard Latrobe. (Eds.) *Public Relations for School Library Media Centers*. Englewood, CO: Libraries Unlimited, 1990.

Seventeen articles about different facets of promoting the school library media program, including definitions of public relations, the library media specialist's attitude and interpersonal skills, stress and public relations, and specific groups to motivate.

36. Loertscher,d. V. *Taxonomies of the School Library Media Program*. Englewood, CO: Libraries Unlimited, 1988.

One of the most outstanding works on elements of the school library media center program. Outlines the roles of media professionals, students, teachers, and administrators in integrating the library media program into the school curriculum. Models for personnel and program evaluation are included in appendices.

37. Pillon, N.b. *Reaching Young People Through Media*. Littleton, CO: Libraries Unlimited, 1983.

Fifteen articles dealing with such topics as reading interests, materials selection, genres, censorship, youth advocacy, and technology .

38. Prostano, Emanuel T. and Joyce S. Prostano. *The School Library Media Center*. 3rd ed. Littleton, CO: Libraries Unlimited, 1982.

Revised in 1987, this book deals with the library media center program development, administration and evaluation. There are also chapters on curriculum integration, media personnel, facilities and furniture, media and equipment, and the budget.

39.   Reichman, Henry. *Censorship and Selection-Issues and Answers for Schools*. Chicago, IL: American Library Association, 1993.

This book addresses the specific problems of intellectual freedom encountered in schools. It discusses issues that are in dispute, selection policies and the law. It also offers possible solutions to complaints.

40.   Report from the White House Office of the Press Secretary on the 1991 White House Conference on Library and Information Services. *Florida Media Quarterly* (Spring 1992), 16-17.

An article summarizing President Bush's comments resulting from the conference in which he pledged executive support for full literacy by the year 2000.

41.   Riggs, D. E. *Strategic Planning for Library Managers*. Phoenix, AZ: Oryx Press, 1984.

A thorough guide for planning for all types of libraries, especially useful in discussing leadership, organization, and evaluation techniques. Especially effective in defining mission statement and distinguishing between goals and objectives.

42.   *School Library Media Annual*. Shirley Aaron and Pat Scales (Eds.) [1983-1987 eds.] and Jane Bandy Smith (Ed.) [1988-1990 eds.] Littleton, CO: Libraries Unlimited.

Each volume contains articles on national and state legislation, professional organizations, government affairs, and publications of note. Individual volumes highlight special issues.

Volume 1: adolescent development, intellectual freedom, certification, instructional radio and television, software evaluations, networking.

Volume 2: lobbying, continuing education, declining enrollment, impact of library media programs on student achievement, telecommunications.

Volume 3: censorship; intellectual freedom committees, copyright concerns, interactive video, microcomputers in schools, ethical considerations.

Volume 4: professionalizing the media profession; planning effective programs; information skills; facilities design; intellectual freedom, censorship, and copyright; managing on-line services.

Volume 5: copyright for new technologies; selection policies and procedures; continuing education; leadership skills; advisory committees; promoting information and inquiry skills.

Volume 6: whole language impact on media, censorship, research on library media centers, updates on automation.

Volume 7: measuring services, developing standards, personnel, flexible scheduling, accreditation, state guidelines, implementing *Information Power*, partnership of NCATE and ALA/AASL.

Volume 8: instructional consulting role, principal's role in creating vision for school library media programs, learning styles, designing effective instruction, contributions of technology, information literacy.

43. Smith, Jane Bandy. *Achieving A Curriculum-Based Library Media Center Program-The Middle School Model for Change.* Chicago, IL: American Library Association, 1995.

This book presents information and practical models for integrating information skills into the school curriculum. This is a sequel to Smith's *Library Media Center Programs for Middle Schools.*

44. *Library Media Center Programs for Middle School: A Curriculum-Based Approach.* Chicago, IL: American Library Association, 1989.

This book presents information on planning and evaluating middle school media programs. It offers procedures in library program development as well as ways of correlating library skills with classroom instruction.

45. Stein, Barbara L. and Risa W. Brown. *Running A School Library Media Center-A How-to-do-it Manual for Librarians.* New York: Neal-Schuman Publishers Inc., 1992.

A practical handbook includes chapters on getting started, administration, ordering and processing materials, cataloging, circulation, maintaining the collection, hiring and working with staff, designing and using the facility, and programming the media center.

46. Sutherland, Zena and M. H. Arbuthnot. *Children and Books.* 7th ed. Glenview, IL: Scott Foresman, 1986.

Chapter One of Part One, "Children and Books Today," discusses the history and direction of children's literature, influences on children's literature, child psychology theories and their application to cognitive development. Chapter Two, "Guiding Children's Book Selection," discusses evaluation standards and examines the elements and range of children's literature. Subsequent chapters provide titles and summaries of recommended literature for various age groups.

47. Talav, Rosemary. *Common Sense Copyright.* New York: McFarland, 1986.

A practical guide to applying copyright laws in school environments, one chapter specifically addressing media centers.

48. Turner, P. M. *Helping Teachers Teach: A School Library Media Specialist's Role.* Littleton, CO: Libraries Unlimited, 1985.

An exploration of the school library media specialist's role as a curriculum consultant, with specific suggestions for methods to help teachers design and evaluate classroom lessons using media resources. Also provides information on professional collection development, instructional materials selection and evaluation, and in-house workshop design. Revised in 1988 and 1993.

49. Van Orden, Phyllis J. *The Collection Program in Schools.* Englewood, CO: Libraries Unlimited, 1988.

A textbook for media professionals on collection development. Divided into three parts: *The Setting* addresses issues, procedures, and policies; *Selection of Materials* addresses selection criteria; and *Administrative Concerns* covers acquisition, maintenance, evaluation, and meeting special needs.

50. Walker, H. T. and P. K. Montgomery. *Teaching Library Media Skills. An Instructional Program for Elementary and Middle School Students.* Littleton, CO: Libraries Unlimited, 1983.

Another good source for using both print and non-print sources to teach library skills. It offers subject-related activities for required and elective subjects as well as discussing the aspects of instruction.

51.   Wehmeyer, L.b. *The School Librarian as Educator.* 2nd ed. Littleton, CO: Libraries Unlimited, 1984.

A text which examines the school library media specialist's role as instructor, offering practical suggestions for library skills instruction and including appendices with games and activities appropriate to both elementary and secondary media centers.

52.   Winn, Patricia. *Integration of the Secondary School Library Media Center into the Curriculum.* Englewood, CO: Libraries Unlimited, 1991.

This title specifically addresses the role of the media specialist in integrating the media program into the curriculum and some methods to use.

53.   Woolls, E. Blanche and David V. Loertscher (Eds.) *The Microcomputer Facility and the School Library Media Specialist.* Chicago, IL: American Library Association, 1986.

This book is a series of essays in four areas: planning the facility, operating the facility, services of the facility, and working with the facility. From district level networks to microcomputers used for circulation, the microcomputer is here presented as a tool to ease the burden of library media management.

54.   Wright, Keith. *The Challenge of Technology-Action Strategies for the School Library Media Specialist.* Chicago. IL: American Library Association, 1993.

Mr. Wright wrote this book because of a concern that technology be used appropriately in education. He addresses the challenges that new technologies have created for the media professional, discusses techniques that schools or districts have used to deal with these challenges, also suggesting ways that school library media specialists can prioritize their growing responsibilities.

55. Yahn, Christina and Ronald Townsend. "Media Centers: Still the Instructional Hub of Schools." *Florida Media Quarterly* 1995: Volume 20, Number 4: 10-11.

An excellent article on the importance of school media centers as the source of integrated learning. The authors stress that Florida's Technology Incentive Grants have expanded technology to the degree that additional human resources are needed to use new technologies effectively in the school.

Sample Test

DIRECTIONS: Read each item and select the best response.

1. **Which of the following is an essential concept in AASL-AECT national guidelines?**
    (Skill 1.1) Average rigor

    A. The school library media program should strive to become an autonomous unit, requiring as little need for interlibrary access as possible.

    B. The school library media program should provide intellectual, social, cultural, and economic freedom of access to information and ideas.

    C. The school library media program should attune itself to the cultural and ethnic demands of its geographical location.

    D. The school library media program should measure its effectiveness by the emphasis it places on the using financial resources to increase its access to current technologies.

2. **The principal is completing the annual report. She needs to include substantive data on use of the media center. In addition to the number of book circulations, she would like to know the proportionate use of the media center's facilities and services by the various grade levels or content areas. This information can most quickly be obtained from:**
    (Skill 1.2) Average rigor

    A. the class scheduling log.

    B. student surveys.

    C. lesson plans.

    D. inventory figures.

3. **National guidelines for school library media programs are generally developed by all of the following except:**
    (Skill 1.2) Easy

    A. AASL.

    B. ALA.

    C. AECT.

    D. NECT.

4. As much as possible, information skills should be taught as:
(Skill 2.1) Easy

A. lessons independent of content studies.

B. lessons to supplement content studies.

C. lessons integrated into content studies.

D. lessons enriched by content studies.

5. When designing a class lesson it is important to include activities that cover a range of learning styles. Virtual field trips and handheld devices would most benefit which learning style?
(Skill 2.2) Rigorous

A. auditory/linguistic

B. logical/mathematical

C. visual

D. kinesthetic

6. Common information skills include all of the following skills except:
(Skill 2.3) Easy

A. tool literacy.

B. visual literacy.

C. validity questioning.

D. evaluation skills.

7. A high school science teacher is about to begin a frog dissection unit. Three students refuse to participate. When asked for assistance, the library media specialist should:
(Skill 3.1) Rigorous

A. work with the teacher to design a replacement unit with print and non-print material on frog anatomy.

B. offer to allow the student to use the library as a study hall during their class time.

C. recommend that the student be sent to another class studying frogs without dissecting.

D. abstain from condoning the student's refusal to work.

8. **Which of the following is the professional organization of Florida school library media specialists?**
    (Skill 3.2) Easy

    A. FSME

    B. FMQ

    C. FIRN

    D. FAME

9. **Current trends in school library media include all of the following except:**
    (Skill 3.3) Average rigor

    A. collaboration.

    B. face to face instruction.

    C. flexible scheduling.

    D. technology integration.

10. **According to AASL/AECT guidelines, in his or her role as *instructional consultant,* the school library media specialist uses his or her expertise to:**
    (Skill 3.4) Average rigor

    A. assist teachers in acquiring information skills which they can incorporate into classroom instruction.

    B. provide access to resource sharing systems.

    C. plan lessons in media production.

    D. provide staff development activities in equipment use

11. **After reading *The Pearl,* a tenth grader asks, "Why can't we start sentences with *and* like John Steinbeck?" This student is showing the ability to:**
    (Skill 4.1) Average rigor

    A. appreciate.

    B. comprehend.

    C. infer.

    D. evaluate.

12. Skills that provide students with the ability to solve problems are known as:
(Skill 4.2) Average rigor

   A. critical thinking skills.

   B. multiple intelligences.

   C. Loertscher's Taxonomies.

   D. authentic learning.

13. Which of the following would be an example of an activity that would use Bloom's taxonomy level of Recall or Knowledge?
(Skill 4.3) Average rigor

   A. Producing a presentation

   B. Retelling a story

   C. Rewriting the ending of a story

   D. React to the author's language or style

14. A kindergarten class has just viewed a video on alligators. The best way to evaluate the suitability of the material for this age group is to:
(Skill 4.4) Rigorous

   A. test the students' ability to recall the main points of the video.

   B. compare this product to other similar products on this content.

   C. observe the body language and verbal comments during the viewing.

   D. ask the children to comment on the quality of the video at the end of the viewing.

15. When creating media for graded class projects, the grade becomes a form of motivation or:
(Skill 4.5) Easy

   A. an external reward.

   B. an internal reward.

   C. an intrinsic reward.

   D. none of the above.

16. **Learning takes place well beyond the walls of the classroom or the hours of the school day. All of the following are ways to accomplish this except:** *(Skill 4.6) Average rigor*

    A. Establish an online library catalog that can be accessed from home

    B. Set a library schedule that matches that of the school day.

    C. Collaborate with public libraries and community colleges.

    D. Invite representatives from other information agencies to promote their programs.

17. **An elementary teacher, planning a unit on the local environment, finds materials that are too global or above his or her students' ability level. The best solution to this problem is to:** *(Skill 5.1) Rigorous*

    A. broaden the scope of the study to emphasize global concerns.

    B. eliminate the unit from the content.

    C. replace the unit with another unit that teaches the same skills.

    D. have the students design their own study materials using media production techniques.

18. **The greatest benefit of learning media production techniques is that it helps:** *(Skill 5.2) Rigorous*

    A. the school reduce the need to purchase commercial products.

    B. the producer clarify his learning objectives.

    C. the teacher individualize instruction.

    D. the school library media specialist integrate information skills.

19. In the production of a teacher/student made audio-visual material, which of the following is NOT a factor in the planning phase?
(Skill 5.3) *Rigorous*

A. stating the objectives.

B. analyzing the audience.

C. determining the purpose.

D. selecting the format.

20. The first step for students designing their own videotape product is:
(Skill 5.3) *Average Rigor*

A. preparing the staging of indoor scenes.

B. assembling a cast.

C. creating a storyboard.

D. calculating a budget.

21. Which of the following is determined first in deciding a media production format?
(Skill 5.4) *Rigor*

A. the size and style of the artwork.

B. the production equipment.

C. the production materials.

D. the method of display.

22. Staff development is most effective when it includes:
(Skill 6.1) *Average rigor*

A. continuing support

B. hand-outs

C. video tutorials

D. stated objectives

23. Staff development activities in the use of materials and equipment are most effective if they:
(Skills 6.1) *Average rigor*

A. are conducted individually as need is expressed.

B. are sequenced in difficulty of operation or use.

C. result in use of the acquired skills in classroom lessons.

D. are evaluated for effectiveness.

24. In assessing learning styles for staff development, consider that adults:
(Skill 6.2) *Rigorous*

A. are less affected by learning environments than children.

B. are more receptive to performing in and in front of groups.

C. learn better when external motivations are guaranteed.

D. demand little feedback.

25. The best way to acclimate a media center volunteer to the workings of the media center is to:
(Skill 6.3) Rigorous

   A. provide the volunteer with a brochure regarding the workings of the media center.
   B. provide the volunteer with a manual that outlines their duties.
   C. provide a hands-on orientation session for the volunteer
   D. provide a video for the volunteer that outlines their duties

26. It is important that library media specialists stay abreast of current trends when designing library programs or selecting resources. Which of the following is NOT a publication classified as an outstanding trend evaluator?
(Skill 7.1) Easy

   A. Education Digest

   B. Phi Delta Kappan

   C. Educational Leadership

   D. Teacher Magazine

27. With regards to the organization of resources in a school, *Florida School Media Programs: A Guide for Excellence* recommends:
(Skill 7.2) Rigorous

   A. all school-owned media should be cataloged and housed in the media center.

   B. certain types of school-owned media should be cataloged and housed in the media center.

   C. all school-owned media should be cataloged regardless of where it is housed.

   D. certain types of school-owned media should be cataloged regardless of where it is housed.

28. To maintain the center's participation in advancing ideas in library media services, a media specialist must dedicate many hours to which of the follow activities?
(Skill 7.2) Average Rigor

A. Read select number of professional resources, including journals, magazines, and research books.

B. Communicate new studies and ideas to classroom teachers.

C. Consult with other library media specialists.

D. All of the above

29. Partners for a school library media program may include:
(Skills 7.4) Easy

A. universities.

B. local businesses.

C. community organizations.

D. all of the above.

30. The first step in planning a training program for untrained support staff is:
(Skills 7.5) Average rigor

A. assessing the employee's existing skills.

B. identifying and prioritizing skills from the job description/evaluation instrument.

C. determining the time schedule for the completion of training.

D. studying the resume and speak to former employers.

31. The Florida DOE's statewide union database is called:
(Skill 7.5) Easy

A. QUICKLINK.

B. DOWNLINK.

C. SUNLINK.

D. SCHOOLLINK.

32. A request from a social studies teacher for the creation of a list of historical fiction titles for a book report assignment is a _____ request.
(Skill 7.6) Rigorous

    A. ready reference

    B. research

    C. specific needs.

    D. complex search

33. Which periodical contains book reviews of currently published children and young adult books?
(Skill 7.7) Rigorous

    A. Phi Delta Kappan

    B. School Library Journal

    C. School Library Media Quarterly

    D. American Teacher

34. Recognition of children's book authors and illustrators is presented by:
(Skill 8.1) Easy

    A. the FAME intellectual freedom committee.

    B. the Sunshine State Book awards.

    C. the Pineapple Press.

    D. the DOE division of media services.

35. The award given for the best children's literature (text) is:
(Skill 8.1) Easy

    A. the Caldecott.

    B. the Newbery.

    C. the Pulitzer.

    D. the Booklist.

36. Which writer composes young adult literature in the fantasy genre?
(Skill 8.2) Rigorous

    A. Stephen King

    B. Piers Anthony

    C. Virginia Hamilton

    D. Phyllis Whitney

37. Which fiction genre do authors Isaac Asimov, Louise Lawrence, and Andre Norton represent?
(Skill 8.2) Rigorous

A. adventure

B. romance

C. science fiction

D. fantasy

38. All of the following are authors of young adult fiction EXCEPT:
(Skill 8.2) Rigorous

A. Paul Zindel.

B. Norma Fox Mazer.

C. S.E. Hinton.

D. Maurice Sendak.

39. All of the following are authors of fantasy except:
(Skill 8.2) Rigorous

A. Ray Bradbury

B. Ursula LeGuin.

C. Piers Anthony.

D. Ann McCaffrey

40. The Caldecott Book Award was given to which book in 2002?
(Skill 8.3) Rigorous

A. *The Three Pigs* by David Wiesner

B. *Had a Little Overcoat* Simms Taback

C. *Golem* by David Wisniewski

D. *Officer Buckle and Gloria* by Peggy Rathmann

41. When selecting materials for a school library media collection which of the following must be considered?
(Skill 8.4) Easy

A. cultural and ethical needs

B. social value

C. intellectual value

D. all of the above

42. An online database that provides print and electronic journal subscriptions is:
(Skill 8.5) Rigorous

A. Kids Connect.

B. KQWeb.

C. EBSCO.

d. NICEM.

43. All of the following are periodical directories except:
(Skill 8.6) Average rigor

A. *Ulrich's.*

B. *TNYT.*

C. *SIRS.*

D. *PAIS.*

44. A statement defining the core principles of a school library media program is called the:
(Skill 9.1) Average rigor

A. mission.

B. policy.

C. procedure.

D. objective.

45. A general statement or outcome that is broken down into specific skills is known as:
(Skill 9.2) Average rigor

A. a policy.

B. a procedure.

C. a goal.

D. an objective.

46. Long range plans should span how many years?
(Skill 9.3) Easy

A. 2 – 4

B. 3 – 5

C. 5 – 10

D. 10 – 15

47. Which of the following is characteristic of a short-range plan?
(Skill 9.4) Average rigor

A. Accomplishable in three or more years

B. Adheres to a rigid set of objectives

C. Identifies immediate cost and funding sources

D. Contains an abstract list of goals

48. The role of the Media Committee or Media Advisory Committee is to assist with all of the following except:
(Skill 9.5) Average rigor

A. determine program direction.

B. evaluate the media specialist.

C. direct budget decisions.

D. collaborate with the media specialist.

49. As a member of the school's curriculum team, the library media specialist's role would include all of the following except:
    (Skill 9.6) Rigorous

    A. ensuring a systematic approach to integrating information skills instruction.

    B. advising staff on appropriate learning styles to meet specific objectives.

    C. advising staff of current trends in curriculum design.

    D. advising staff of objectives design for specific content areas.

50. Which of the following is an example of quantitative data that would be used to evaluate a school library media program?
    (Skill 10.1) Average rigor

    A. Personnel evaluations

    B. Usage statistics

    C. Surveys

    D. Interviews

51. An accredited elementary school has maintained an acceptable number of items in its print collection for ten years. In the evaluation review, this fact is evidence of both:
    (Skill 10.1) Rigorous

    A. diagnostic and projective standards.

    B. diagnostic and quantitative standards.

    C. projective and quantitative standards.

    D. projective and qualitative standards.

52. **In preparation for submitting the media program's budget to the proper administrators, a media specialist should include all of the following except:**
(Skill 10.2) Rigorous

A. Inventory logs to inform of lost, stolen, or damaged materials.

B. List of books borrowed by the valedictorian to display types of materials that lead to successful performance at school.

C. Class scheduling logs to show frequency of integration of classroom studies with the library media program.

D. None of the above

53. **Ongoing evaluation is necessary to produce a quality media program. Which of the following can evaluation be used for?**
(Skill 10.3) Rigorous

A. lobbying for budgetary or personnel support

B. to make changes to the use of the media center materials

C. to determine circulation regulations

D. all of the above

54. **In formulating an estimated collection budget consider all of the following except:**
(Skill 11.1) Rigorous

A. attrition by loss, damage, or age.

B. the maximum cost of item replacement.

C. the number of students served.

D. the need for expansion to meet minimum guidelines.

55. **The most appropriate means of obtaining extra funds for library media programs is:**
(Skill 11.2) Average rigor

A. having candy sales.

B. conducting book fairs.

C. charging fines.

D. soliciting donations.

56. **To communicate budgetary needs and concerns, the best option for the media specialist is to:**
(Skill 11.3) Rigorous

A. Send memos to staff

B. Determine needs based upon their own observations.

C. Work closely with the media advisory committee.

D. None of the above

57. **In a school with one full-time library media assistant (clerk), which of the following are responsibilities of the assistant?**
(Skill 12.1) Average rigor

A. selecting and ordering titles for the print collection.

B. performing circulation tasks and processing new materials.

C. inservicing teachers on the integration of media materials into the school curriculum.

D. planning and implementing programs to involve parents and community.

58. **Which of the following tasks should a volunteer NOT be asked to perform?**
(Skill 12.1) Average rigor

A. decorating bulletin boards.

B. demonstrating use of retrieval systems.

C. maintaining bookkeeping records.

D. fundraising.

59. **AASL/AECT guidelines recommend that student library aides be:**
(Skill 12.1) *Average rigor*

A. rewarded with grades or certificates for their service.

B. allowed to assist only during free time.

C. allowed to perform paraprofessional duties.

D. assigned tasks that relate to maintaining the atmosphere of the media center.

60. **A school with 500 – 749 students should have how many media specialists?**
(Skill 12.2) *Easy*

A. 1 part-time media specialist

B. 1 full time media specialist

C. 2 full time media specialist

D. no media specialist required

61. **The most efficient method of evaluating support staff is to:**
(Skill 12.3) *Average rigor*

A. administer a written test.

B. survey faculty whom they serve.

C. observe their performance.

D. obtain verbal confirmation during an employee interview.

62. **Which of the following is a library policy, not a procedure?**
(Skill 13.1) *Rigorous*

A. providing a vehicle for the circulation of audio-visual equipment.

B. setting guidelines for collection development.

C. determining the method for introducing an objective into the school improvement plan.

D. setting categorical limits on operating expenses.

63. **A policy is:**
    (Skill 13.1) Easy

    A. a course of action taken to execute a plan.

    B. a written statement of principle used to guarantee a management practice.

    C. a statement of core values of an organization.

    D. a regulation concerning certification.

64. **Collection development policies are developed to accomplish all of the following except:**
    (Skill 13.2) Rigorous

    A. guarantee users freedom to access information.

    B. recognize the needs and interests of users.

    C. coordinate selection criteria and budget concerns.

    D. recognize rights of individuals or groups to challenge these policies.

65. **Which of the following should participate in the development of local policies and procedures?**
    (Skill 13.3) Average rigor

    A. teacher

    B. student

    C. parents

    D. all of the above

66. **A library procedures manual should contain which of the following?**
    (Skill 13.4) Average rigor

    A. mission

    B. specific media policies

    C. specific media procedures

    D. all of the above

67. **Current trends in school library media include all of the following except:**
    (Skill 13.5) Average rigor

    A. collaboration.

    B. face to face instruction.

    C. flexible scheduling.

    D. technology integration.

68. **Contemporary library media design models should consider which of the following an optional need?**
(Skill 14.1) Rigorous

A. flexibility of space to allow for reading, viewing, and listening.

B. space for large group activities such as district meetings, standardized testing, and lectures.

C. traffic flow patterns for entrance and exit from the media center as well as easy movement within the center.

D. adequate and easy to rearrange storage areas for the variety of media formats and packaging style of modern materials.

69. **The most important consideration in the design of a new school library media center is:**
(Skill 14.1) Average rigor

A. the goals of the library media center program.

B. the location of the facility on the school campus.

C. state standards for facilities use.

D. the demands of current technologies.

70. **Factors that influence the atmosphere of a library media center contain all of the following except:**
(Skill 14.2) Rigorous

A. aesthetic appearance.

B. acoustical ceiling and floor coverings.

C. size of the media center.

D. proximity to classrooms.

71. **MARC is the acronym for:**
(Skill 15.1) Average Rigor

A. Mobile Accessible Recorded Content

B. Machine Accessible Readable Content

C. Machine Readable Content

D. Mobile Accessible Readable Content

72. **In which bibliographic field should information concerning the format of an audio-visual material appear?**
(Skill 15.2) Rigorous

A. Material specific details.

B. Physical description.

C. Notes.

D. Standard numbers.

73. **In what area of a bibliographic record can the name of the author be found?**
    (Skill 15.2) Average rigor

    A. physical description area

    B. publication area

    C. terms of availability area.

    D. title and statement of responsibility area

74. **Which of the following is not a component of a bibliographic record?**
    (Skill 15.2) Rigorous

    A. Notes

    B. Call number

    C. Cover image

    D. Physical description area

75. **OCLC is the acronym for:**
    (Skill 15.3) Average rigor

    A. Online Computer Library Center.

    B. Online Computer Library Catalog.

    C. Online Computer Library Conference.

    D. Online Computer Library Content.

76. **AACR2 is the acronym for:**
    (Skill 15.3) Easy

    A. Anglo-American Cataloging Rules Second Edition.

    B. American Association of Cataloging Rules Second Edition.

    C. American Association of Content Rules Second Edition.

    D. Anglo-American Content Rules Second Edition.

77 **In MARC records the title information can be found under which tag?**
    (Skill 15.3) Rigorous

    A. 130

    B. 245

    C. 425

    D. 520

78. Following a standard set of international rules, *Anglo-American Cataloguing Rules*, enables users to locate materials equally well in all libraries that subscribe to these rules. To maintain this integrity, it is necessary for catalogers to do all of the following except:
(Skill 15.4) Rigorous

A. Recognize an International Standard Bibliographic Description (ISBD) that establishes the order in which bibliographic elements will appear in catalog entries.

B. Note changes that occur after each five years review of ISBD.

C. Agree to catalog all materials using the AACR standards.

D. Note changes that occur after each five year review of AACR.

79. The most efficient method of assessing which students are users or non-users of the library media center is reviewing:
(Skill 16.1) Average rigor

A. patron circulation records.

B. needs assessment surveys of students.

C. monthly circulation statistics.

D. the accession book for the current year.

80. Libraries have changed from the stuffy no-talking zones of the past to bright, interactive, and frequently noisy epicenters of information at the heart of many schools. Which scenario best describes such a place?
(Skill 16.2) Rigorous

A. The media specialist collaborates with teachers to integrate information skills into the curriculum.

B. In lieu of tables, cubicles are set up throughout the media center for students to work without disturbance.

C. When in need of assistance, teachers must submit a formal request to the media specialist.

D. The media center has set its hours of operation to that of the school day. It is not open for early morning or after school usage.

81. **Which of the following are examples of ways to promote the school library media programs?**
    (Skill 16.3) Easy

    A. Attend school board meetings.

    B. Serve on the school's curriculum committee.

    C. Invite school board members to media planning meetings.

    D. All of the above

82. **Which of the following is NOT one of three general criteria for selection of all materials?**
    (Skill 17.1) Average rigor

    A. authenticity

    B. appeal

    C. appropriateness

    D. allocation

83. **Collection development principles in *Florida School Media Programs: A Guide for Excellence* recommend that:**
    (Skill 17.2) Average rigor

    A. only materials housed in the media center should be catalogued.

    B. only materials purchased with media center funds should be catalogued.

    C. all school-owned media resources should be catalogued in the media collection.

    D. materials already held in the district media catalog should not be purchased.

84. **Policies that determine procedures for copyright laws and reproduction of materials are generally determined at which level?**
    (Skill 17.3) Average rigor

    A. grade level

    B. school level

    C. community level

    D. district level

85. When determining a specific piece of equipment to purchase, the school library media specialist should first consult:
(Skill 17.4) Average rigor

A. local vendors for a demonstration.

B. reviews in technology periodicals.

C. manufacturers' catalogs for specifications.

D. the state bid list for price

86. When selecting print or non-print materials all of the following are potential sources of current information except:
(Skill 17.5) Easy

A. catalogs from publishers and vendors.

B. lists of award winners.

C. professional journals.

D. Internet search results.

87. Books with strong picture support, familiar language patterns, and use of cuing systems are best for which group of students?
(Skill 17.6) Average rigor

A. K-2

B. 3-5

C. 6-8

D. 9-12

88. Which of these publications does not contain reviews for various types of publications:
(Skill 17.6) Average rigor

A. School Library Journal.

B. Booklist.

C. Media Center Review.

D. The Horn Book.

89. Comparing holdings records to bibliographies, conducting user surveys and examining resources are all procedures that may provide data for a:
(Skill 17.7) Average rigor

A. circulation evaluation.

B. collection evaluation.

C. program evaluation.

D. school evaluation.

90. **The practice of examining the quantity and quality of the school library media resource collection which provides a "snapshot" of the collection is called:**
(Skill 17.7) Easy

   A. collection development.

   B. collection maintenance.

   C. collection mapping.

   D. weeding.

91. **Circulation limitations include:**
(Skill 18.1) Average rigor

   A. the number of items circulable to an individual borrower.

   B. the need for theft detection devices.

   C. overnight loans for special items.

   D. limits on circulation of reserve collections.

92. **When automating a library catalog it is important to consider which of the following prior to set up?**
(Skill 18.2) Easy

   A. technical requirements

   B. loan period

   C. patron limitations

   D. color of spine labels

93. **The procedures for conducting an inventory of the media collection include all of the following except:**
(Skill 18.3) Rigorous

   A. Determining the cost of the inventory.

   B. Determining when the inventory will be conducted.

   C. Determining who will conduct the inventory.

   D. Determining if each item matches the information in the holding records.

94. To ensure the collection meets student needs which steps should the media specialist take?
(Skill 18.4) Rigorous

A. Develop specific processes for evaluating and updating the collection.

B. Have access to up-to-date collection monitoring and evaluation tools and reviewing resources.

C. Ensure that the media collection adheres to similar bibliographic lists.

D. Support the circulation of resources by sharing information with teachers and allowing them to preview new resources as well as take part in the selection process.

95. The process of discarding worn or outdated books and materials is known as:
(Skill 18.5) Easy

A. weeding.

B. inventory.

C. collection mapping.

D. eliminating.

96. Which of these Dewey Decimal classifications should be weeded most often?
(Skill 18.5) Rigorous

A. 100s

B. 500s

C. 700s

D. Biographies

97. An acronym that is often used to remind media specialists of the steps to weeding a collection is:
(Skill 18.5) Average rigor

A. WEAR.

B. MUSTIE.

C. ABCD.

D. RIPPED.

98. **Collaborative partnerships with staff can take on many forms. All of the following are examples except:**
    (Skill 19.1) Rigorous

    A. serving on curriculum development committees.

    B. viewing the school's curriculum and creating lessons.

    C. assisting teachers in planning, designing, and teaching lessons.

    D. assisting teachers and students with the use of new technologies.

99. **A good leader should:**
    (Skill 19.2) Average rigor

    A. delegate responsibility.

    B. show respect for colleagues.

    C. engage in continuing education.

    D. all of the above.

100. **To foster the collaborative process the media specialist must possess all of the following skills except:**
     (Skill 19.3) Easy

     A. leadership.

     B. flexibility.

     C. perversion.

     D. persistence.

101. **Florida State Law 231.15 identifies a school library media specialist as:**
     (Skill 20.1) Rigorous

     A. a licensed support person.

     B. an instructional employee.

     C. a non-instructional employee.

     D. an administrator /supervisor.

102. **The federal law enacted by Congress in December 2000 that imposed specific Internet restrictions on schools that receive Federal E-rate funding is known as:**
     (Skill 20.2) Average rigor

     A. CIP.

     B. CIPA.

     C. SIP.

     D. AUP.

103. Which of the following has made the greatest impact on school library media centers in the last decade? *(Skill 21.1) Average rigor*

    A. censorship

    B. emerging technologies

    C. learning style research

    D. state funding reductions

104. Which of the following is NOT an expert in child development? *(Skill 21.2) Rigorous*

    A. Lawrence Kohlberg

    B. James Naisbitt

    C. Jean Piaget

    D. Erik Erikson

105. All of the following organizations serve school libraries except: *(Skill 22.1) Average rigor*

    A. AASL.

    B. AECT.

    C. ALCT.

    D. ALA.

106. Which version of *Information Power* was published in 1998? *(Skill 22.2) Easy*

    A. *Information Power: The Role of the School Library Media Program*

    B. *Information Power: A Review of Research*

    C. *Information Power: Guidelines for School Library Media Programs*

    D. *Information Power: Building Partnerships for Learning*

107. According to *Information Power*, which of the following is NOT a responsibility of the school library media specialist? *(Skill 22.2) Rigorous*

    A. maintaining and repairing equipment

    B. instructing educators and parents in the use of library media resources

    C. providing efficient retrieval systems for materials and equipment

    D. planning and implementing the library media center budget

108. **Which of the following is the best description of the ALA recommendations for certification for a school library media specialist?** *(Skill 22.3) Average rigor*

    A. a bachelor's degree in any content area plus 30 hours of library/information science

    B. a master's degree from an accredited Educational Media program

    C. a bachelor's degree in library/ information science and a master's degree in any field of education

    D. a master's degree from an accredited Library and Information Studies program

109. **The TAXONOMIES OF THE SCHOOL LIBRARY MEDIA PROGRAM outlines eleven levels of school library media specialists' involvement with curriculum and instruction and was developed by:** *(Skill 22.3) Rigorous*

    A. Eisenberg.

    B. Bloom.

    C. Loertscher.

    D. Lance.

110. **The Right to Read Statement was issued by:** *(Skill 23.1) Rigorous*

    A. AECT.

    B. ALA.

    C. NCTE.

    D. NICEM.

111. **In the landmark U.S. Supreme Court ruling in favor of Pico, the court's opinion established that:** *(Skill 23.2) Rigorous*

    A. library books, being optional not required reading, could not be arbitrarily removed by school boards.

    B. school boards have the same jurisdiction over library books as they have over textbooks.

    C. the intent to remove pervasively vulgar material is the same as the intent to deny free access to ideas.

    D. First Amendment challenges in regards to library books are the responsibility of appeals courts.

112. When creating a schedule for a school library media center the type of schedule that maximizes access to resources is a:
(Skill 23.3) Easy

   A. fixed schedule.

   B. open schedule.

   C. partial fixed schedule.

   D. flexible schedule.

113. The school library media center should be an inviting space that encourages learning. To accomplish this the school library media specialist should do all of the following except:
(Skill 23.3) Average rigor

   A. collaborate with school staff and students.

   B. create a schedule where each class comes to the media center each week for instruction.

   C. arrange materials so that they are easy to locate.

   D. promote the program as a wonderful place for learning.

114. The Position Statement on Flexible Scheduling was developed by:
(Skill 23.3) Average rigor

   A. AASL.

   B. ALA.

   C. AECT.

   D. SLMA.

115. All of the following are benefits of interlibrary loan except:
(Skill 23.4) Rigorous

   A. maximizing the use media center funds.

   B. providing a wider range of resources available for patrons.

   C. building partnerships with outside agencies.

   D. eliminating the need for media assistants.

116. Instructional materials are evolving into all of the following formats except:
(Skill 23.5) Average rigor

   A. ebooks.

   B. online magazines.

   C. audio cassettes.

   D. interactive software.

117. Which professional journal is published by the American Association of School Librarians? *(Skill 24.1) Average rigor*

   A. *School Library Media Research*

   B. *Library Trends*

   C. *Library Power*

   D. *Voices of Youth Advocate*

118. When reviewing research information a media specialist should consider all of the following questions except: *(Skill 24.2)*

   A. What was the topic of the report?

   B. How does the information found in this project fit what is known?

   C. How was the research completed?

   D. All of the above

119. According to research on promotion techniques and support for library media programs, their staunchest ally must be the: *(Skill 24.3) Easy*

   A. teaching faculty.

   B. student body.

   C. district media supervisor.

   D. school principal.

120. When a suspected infringement of copyright is brought to the attention of the school library media specialist, he or she should follow certain procedures. Which of the following is not one of the procedures? *(Skill 25.1) Rigorous*

    A. If an instance is verified, tactfully inform the violator of the specific criteria to use so that future violations can be avoided. Presented properly, the information will be accepted as constructive.

    B. Determine if a violation has in effect occurred. Never accuse or report alleged instances to a higher authority without verification.

    C. If advice is unheeded and further infractions occur, bring them to the attention of the teacher's supervisor (e.g., a team leader or department chair) who can handle the matter as an evaluation procedure.

    D. If further infractions persist after the teacher's supervisor has been notified then it is necessary to consult the proper authorities to handle the situation.

121. When a parent complains about the content of a specific title in a library media collection, the library media specialist's first course of action in responding to the complaint is to: *(Skill 25.2) Rigorous*

    A. remove the title from the shelf and purge it from both the catalog and the shelf list.

    B. place the book in reserve status for circulation at parent request only.

    C. submit the complaint to a district review committee.

    D. explain the principles of intellectual freedom to the complaining parent.

122. The responsibility for appointing a reconsideration committee to examine a challenged material belongs to: *(Skill 25.2) Average rigor*

    A. the school superintendent.

    B. the district media supervisor.

    C. the school principal.

    D. the school library media specialist.

123. A student looks for a specific title on domestic violence. When he learns it is overdue, he asks the library media specialist to tell him the borrower's name. The library media specialist should first:
(Skill 25.3) Rigorous

   A. readily reveal the borrower's name.

   B. suggest he look for the book in another library.

   C. offer to put the boy's name on reserve pending the book's return.

   D. offer to request an interlibrary loan.

124. Which of the following is the least effective way of communicating school library media policies, procedures, and rules to media center patrons?
(Skill 17.8) Average Rigor

   A. announcements made in faculty and parent support group meetings

   B. a published faculty procedures manual

   C. written guidelines in the student handbook or special media handbill

   D. a videotape orientation viewed over the school's closed circuit television system

125. Which of the following media should be included in the school library media center's resource collection?
(Skill 17.4) Rigorous

   A. audio recordings

   B. periodicals

   C. online resources

   D. all of the above

Answer Key:

1. B	33. B	65. D	97. B
2. A	34. B	66. D	98. B
3. D	35. B	67. B	99. D
4. D	36. B	68. B	100. C
5. D	37. C	69. A	101. B
6. B	38. D	70. C	102. B
7. A	39. A	71. C	103. B
8. D	40. A	72. C	104. B
9. B	41. D	73. D	105. C
10. D	42. C	74. C	106. D
11. D	43. B	75. A	107. A
12. A	44. A	76. A	108. D
13. B	45. C	77. B	109. C
14. C	46. B	78. D	110. C
15. A	47. C	79. A	111. A
16. B	48. B	80. A	112. D
17. D	49. D	81. D	113. B
18. B	50. B	82. D	114. A
19. D	51. B	83. C	115. D
20. C	52. B	84. D	116. C
21. D	53. D	85. C	117. A
22. A	54. B	86. D	118. D
23. C	55. B	87. A	119. D
24. B	56. C	88. C	120. D
25. C	57. B	89. B	121. D
26. D	58. C	90. C	122. B
27. C	59. A	91. B	123. C
28. D	60. B	92. A	124. A
29. D	61. C	93. A	125. D
30. B	62. B	94. C	
31. C	63. B	95. A	
32. C	64. C	96. B	

Rigor Table

	Easy %20	Average Rigor %40	Rigorous %40
Question #	3, 4, 6, 8, 15, 26, 29, 31, 34, 35, 41, 46, 60, 63, 76, 81, 86, 90, 92, 95, 100, 106, 112, 119	1, 2, 9, 10, 11, 12, 13, 16, 20, 22, 23, 28, 30, 43, 44, 45, 47, 48, 50, 55, 57, 58, 59, 61, 65, 66, 67, 69, 71, 73, 75, 79, 82, 83, 84, 85, 87, 88, 89, 91, 97, 99, 102, 103, 105, 108, 113, 114, 116, 117, 122, 124	5, 7, 14, 17, 18, 19, 21, 24, 25, 27, 32, 33, 36, 37, 38, 39, 40, 42, 49, 51, 52, 53, 54, 56, 62, 64, 68, 70, 72, 74, 77, 78, 80, 93, 94, 96, 98, 101, 104, 107, 109, 110, 111, 115, 118, 120, 121, 123, 125

Rationales with Sample Questions

1. **Which of the following is an essential concept in AASL-AECT national guidelines?**
   (Skill 1.1) Average rigor

   a. The school library media program should strive to become an autonomous unit, requiring as little need for interlibrary access as possible.
   b. The school library media program should provide intellectual, social, cultural, and economic freedom of access to information and ideas.
   c. The school library media program should attune itself to the cultural and ethnic demands of its geographical location.
   d. The school library media program should measure its effectiveness by the emphasis it places on the using financial resources to increase its access to current technologies.

Answer: b. The school library media program should provide intellectual, social, cultural, and economic freedom of access to information and ideas.

As identified in the mission statement of ALA's *Information Power* publications, the school library media program should be designed to provide a wide range of access to information and ideas as found in Option B. The school library media program should strive to be an integral part of the school environment and should not limit its resources to just those pertaining to a specific culture or location.

2. The principal is completing the annual report. She needs to include substantive data on use of the media center. In addition to the number of book circulations, she would like to know the proportionate use of the media center's facilities and services by the various grade levels or content areas. This information can most quickly be obtained from:
(Skill 1.2) Average rigor

a. the class scheduling log.
b. student surveys.
c. lesson plans.
d. inventory figures.

Answer: a. the class scheduling log

The schedule is one of the best tools for determining how the media center's facilities are being used. Often the schedule is broken down by the various areas in the media center. Teachers may schedule the specific area(s) they need. This makes Option A the most appropriate answer.

3. National guidelines for school library media programs are generally developed by all of the following except:
(Skill 1.2) Easy

a. AASL.
b. ALA.
c. AECT.
d. NECT.

Answer: d. NECT.

AASL, ALA, and AECT assist with developing guidelines for school library media centers. Option D is the most appropriate answer.

4.   As much as possible, information skills should be taught as:
        (Skill 2.1) Easy

a.   lessons independent of content studies.
b.   lessons to supplement content studies.
c.   lessons integrated into content studies.
d.   lessons enriched by content studies.

Answer: d. lessons integrated into content studies.

The current Information on literacy curriculum is thoroughly integrated into the core content areas. It stresses the correlation between the National Information Power Standards, The Florida Student Information Literacy Descriptors and The Sunshine State Standards. Therefore, Option D is the correct answer.

5 .   When designing a class lesson it is important to include activities that cover a range of learning styles. Virtual field trips and handheld devices would most benefit which learning style?
        (Skill 2.2) Rigorous

a.   auditory/linguistic
b.   logical/mathematical
c.   visual
d.   kinesthetic

Answer: d. kinesthetic

Students with this learning style benefit most from hands on, tactile experiences. Option D is the most appropriate answer.

6.   Common information skills include all of the following skills except:
        (Skill 2.3) Easy

a.   tool literacy.
b.   visual literacy.
c.   validity questioning.
d.   evaluation skills.

Answer: b. visual literacy.

Basic information skills include tool literacy, searching skills, evaluation skills, questioning skills and organization skills. Visual literacy is not considered an information skill. This makes Option B. the most appropriate answer.

7.   A high school science teacher is about to begin a frog dissection unit. Three students refuse to participate. When asked for assistance, the library media specialist should:
(Skill 3.1) Rigorous

a.   work with the teacher to design a replacement unit with print and non-print material on frog anatomy.
b.   offer to allow the student to use the library as a study hall during their class time.
c.   recommend that the student be sent to another class studying frogs without dissecting.
d.   abstain from condoning the student's refusal to work.

Answer: a. work with the teacher to design a replacement unit with print and non-print material on frog anatomy.

To ensure that students learn the material that would be covered by such an activity there should be an alternate plan for instruction. The school library media specialist could play a crucial role in helping teachers to develop alternate plans. Option A is the best answer.

8.   Which of the following is the professional organization of Florida school library media specialists?
(Skill 3.2) Easy

a.   FSME
b.   FMQ
c.   FIRN
d.   FAME

Answer: d. FAME

FAME stands for Florida Association for Media in Education, which is the professional organization for school library media specialists, making Option D the most appropriate answer. The FIRN is the Florida Information Resource Network.

9. **Current trends in school library media include all of the following except:**
(*Skill 3.3*) *Average rigor*

a. collaboration.
b. face to face instruction.
c. flexible scheduling.
d. technology integration.

Answer: b. face to face instruction

Face to face instruction is not one of the current trends in school library media. Collaboration, flexible scheduling, and technology integration are some of the trends affecting school library media programs.

10. **According to AASL/AECT guidelines, in his or her role as *instructional consultant*, the school library media specialist uses his or her expertise to:**
(*Skill 3.4*) *Average rigor*

a. assist teachers in acquiring information skills which they can incorporate into classroom instruction.
b. provide access to resource sharing systems.
c. plan lessons in media production.
d. provide staff development activities in equipment use.

Answer: d. provide staff development activities in equipment use.

As an instructional consultant, the school library media specialist does provide staff development activities. Providing access is part of the role of program administrator. Assisting teachers and planning lessons is part of the teaching role of a media specialist. This makes Option D the most appropriate answer.

11. After reading *The Pearl,* a tenth grader asks, "Why can't we start sentences with *and* like John Steinbeck?" This student is showing the ability to:
(*Skill 4.1*) *Average rigor*

a. appreciate.
b. comprehend.
c. infer.
d. evaluate.

Answer: d. evaluate.

Under the description of the Bloom's Taxonomy level of evaluation students that demonstrate this level of higher order thinking are able to
- make choices based upon well thought out arguments,
- compare ideas,
- and recognize subjectivity.

12. Skills that provide students with the ability to solve problems are known as:
(*Skill 4.2*) *Average rigor*

a. critical thinking skills.
b. multiple intelligences.
c. Loertscher's Taxonomies.
d. authentic learning.

Answer: a. critical thinking skills

Critical thinking skills are the skills students need to find solutions to complex problems. This makes Option A the most appropriate answer.

13.   **Which of the following would be an example of an activity that would use Bloom's taxonomy level of Recall or Knowledge?**
      (Skill 4.3) Average rigor

a.   Producing a presentation
b.   Retelling a story
c.   Rewriting the ending of a story
d.   React to the author's language or style

Answer: b. Retelling a story.

The recall or knowledge level of Bloom's taxonomy focuses upon the repetition of facts. This makes Option B the most appropriate answer. All of the others require students to use higher order skills to accomplish the task.

14.   **A kindergarten class has just viewed a video on alligators. The best way to evaluate the suitability of the material for this age group is to:**
      (Skill 4.4) Rigorous

a.   test the students' ability to recall the main points of the video.
b.   compare this product to other similar products on this content.
c.   observe the body language and verbal comments during the viewing.
d.   ask the children to comment on the quality of the video at the end of the viewing.

Answer: c. observe the body language and verbal comments during the viewing

Students may be able to view any video and be able to recall facts, but suitability for a particular age may best be evaluated by how well students respond to the video as it is being viewed. This makes Option C the most appropriate answer.

15. **When creating media for graded class projects, the grade becomes a form of motivation or:**
(Skill 4.5) Easy

a. an external reward
b. an internal reward
c. an intrinsic reward
d. none of the above

Answer: a. external reward

The correct answer is Option A, external reward. Internal and intrinsic rewards are one in the same.

16. **Learning takes place well beyond the walls of the classroom or the hours of the school day. All of the following are ways to accomplish this except:**
(Skill 4.6) Average rigor

a. Establish an online library catalog that can be accessed from home
b. Set a library schedule that matches that of the school day.
c. Collaborate with public libraries and community colleges.
d. Invite representatives from other information agencies to promote their programs.

Answer: b. Set a library schedule that matches that of the school day.

To foster lifelong learning libraries should strive to extend their hours of operation to accommodate students who may need to have access to resources before or after school.

17. **An elementary teacher, planning a unit on the local environment, finds materials that are too global or above his or her students' ability level. The best solution to this problem is to:**
(Skill 5.1) Rigorous

a.   broaden the scope of the study to emphasize global concerns.
b.   eliminate the unit from the content.
c.   replace the unit with another unit that teaches the same skills.
d.   have the students design their own study materials using media production techniques.

Answer: d. have the students design their own study materials using media production techniques.

When commercial materials cannot be found to meet student needs, the best alternative is to have students design their own materials. By designing and creating their own materials students tend to develop a deeper understanding of the material.

18. **The greatest benefit of learning media production techniques is that it helps:**
(Skill 5.2) Rigorous

a.   the school reduce the need to purchase commercial products.
b.   the producer clarify his learning objectives.
c.   the teacher individualize instruction.
d.   the school library media specialist integrate information skills.

Answer: b. the producer clarify his learning objectives.

The greatest benefit of media production generally comes to the producer. This is the person in charge of the production. To make the production most effective the producer must clarify his or her goals and specifically outline the learning objectives. This makes Option B the most appropriate answer.

19. In the production of a teacher/student-made audio-visual material, which of the following is NOT a factor in the planning phase? *(Skill 5.3) Rigorous*

   a. stating the objectives.
   b. analyzing the audience.
   c. determining the purpose.
   d. selecting the format.

Answer: d. selecting the format.

In planning for any audio-visual materials, as in planning any student work, it is important to determine the purpose, analyze the audience, and state the objectives. While selecting the format is important, it is not one of the first steps that must be taken.

20. The first step for students designing their own videotape product is: *(Skill 5.3) Average Rigor*

   a. preparing the staging of indoor scenes.
   b. assembling a cast.
   c. creating a storyboard.
   d. calculating a budget.

Answer: c. creating a storyboard.

The correct answer is Option C. A storyboard is a series of panels that provide a rough sketch of each scene in a video.

21. Which of the following is determined first in deciding a media production format? *(Skill 5.4) Rigor*

   a. the size and style of the artwork.
   b. the production equipment.
   c. the production materials.
   d. the method of display.

Answer: d. the method of display.

How the media will be displayed will depend upon the format of the media. It will determine the size and style of the artwork and the equipment that would be used. It is Option D, the method of display that will determine the production format.

22.   **Staff development is most effective when it includes:**
        (Skill 6.1) Average rigor

a.   continuing support
b.   hand-outs
c.   video tutorials
d.   stated objectives

Answer: a. continuing support

While the other options are important to consider when providing staff development, it is the provision of continuing support that ensures the information learned will used to its fullest potential. Option A is the most appropriate answer.

23.   **Staff development activities in the use of materials and equipment are most effective if they:**
        (Skills 6.1) Average rigor

a.   are conducted individually as need is expressed.
b.   are sequenced in difficulty of operation or use.
c.   result in use of the acquired skills in classroom lessons.
d.   are evaluated for effectiveness.

Answer: c. result in use of the acquired skills in classroom lessons.

Option C is the most appropriate answer. The ultimate goal of most staff development activities is use or integration in the classroom.

24.   **In assessing learning styles for staff development, consider that adults:**
        (Skill 6.2) Rigorous

a.   are less affected by learning environment than children.
b.   are more receptive to performing in and in front of groups.
c.   learn better when external motivations are guaranteed.
d.   demand little feedback.

Answer: b. are more receptive to performing in front of groups.

Adult learners often need as much feedback on performance as their students would, especially when learning new skills. They are affected by their learning environments and will still perform even if there are no external rewards. It is Option B that is the correct answer. Adult learners are more receptive to performing in front of groups.

25. **The best way to acclimate a media center volunteer to the workings of the media center is to:**
   (Skill 6.3) Rigorous

a. provide the volunteer with a brochure regarding the workings of the media center.
b. provide the volunteer with a manual that outlines their duties.
c. provide a hands-on orientation session for the volunteer
d. provide a video for the volunteer that outlines their duties

Answer: c. provide a hands-on orientation session for the volunteer

Volunteers receive the greatest training benefit when they are provided with hands-on training. This makes Option C the most appropriate answer.

26. **It is important that library media specialists stay abreast of current trends when designing library programs or selecting resources. Which of the following is NOT a publication classified as an outstanding trend evaluator?**
   (Skill 7.1) Easy

a. *Education Digest*

b. *Phi Delta Kappan*

c. *Educational Leadership*

d. *Teacher Magazine*

Answer: d. *Teacher Magazine*

Teacher Magazine is a good source for grant information, but the others are better known for evaluating trends in education. This makes Option D the most appropriate answer.

27. **With regards to the organization of resources in a school, *Florida School Media Programs: A Guide for Excellence* recommends: (Skill 7.2) Rigorous**

a. all school-owned media should appear in the media center catalog and housed in the media center.
b. certain types of school-owned media should appear in the media center catalog and housed in the media center.
c. all school-owned media appear in the media center catalog regardless of where it is housed.
d. certain types of school-owned media should appear in the media center catalog regardless of where it is housed.

Answer: c. all school-owned media should be cataloged regardless of where it is housed.

All materials should appear in the media center catalog regardless of where they are housed so that there may be a central search location. Having all the information in one place makes it easier for staff to find resources.

28. **To maintain the center's participation in advancing ideas in library media services, a media specialist must dedicate many hours to which of the follow activities? (Skill 7.2) Average Rigor**

a. Read select number of professional resources, including journals, magazines, and research books.
b. Communicate new studies and ideas to classroom teachers.
c. Consult with other library media specialists.
d. All of the above

Answer: D. All of the above.

Each of these activities will assure a media specialist's programming follows current trends in research and education. While professional resources are important, there is too much information to reading all of them an efficient use of time. A media specialist should also be involved in his or her learning community, whether consulting with other media specialists or briefing teachers with new research and techniques for integrating media programs into the classroom.

29.   Partners for a school library media program may include:
(Skills 7.4) Easy

a.   universities.
b.   local businesses.
c.   community organizations.
d.   all of the above.

Answer: d. all of the above

Universities, local businesses, and community organizations are all viable partners for a media program. Universities may provide additional training for staff or open their resource catalog for use by local school districts. Local businesses often donate funds, equipment or professional expertise to local schools. Community organizations work to turn students into strong community leaders by providing programs and awards.

30.   The first step in planning a training program for untrained support staff is:
(Skills 7.5) Average rigor

a.   assessing the employee's existing skills.
b.   identifying and prioritizing skills from the job description/ evaluation instrument.
c.   determining the time schedule for the completion of training.
d.   studying the resume and speak to former employers.

Answer: b. identifying and prioritizing skills from the job description/ evaluation instrument.

The best place to begin planning a training program for untrained support staff is to take a look at the job description or evaluation instrument and determine the skills that need to be learned. From there one could study the employee's resume, assess his or her skills and plan a schedule for training

31.   The Florida DOE's statewide union database is called:
       (Skill 7.5) Easy

a.   QUICKLINK.
b.   DOWNLINK.
c.   SUNLINK.
d.   SCHOOLLINK.

Answer: c. SUNLINK

In 1992 the Florida Department of Education's School Media Services Division introduced SUNLINK, a CD-ROM union database, which facilitates interlibrary loan throughout the state's public schools. Each project school was provided funds in 1995-96 to purchase a dedicated computer for the SUNLINK program. SUNLINK now provides online access to resources.

32.   A request from a social studies for the creation of a list of historical fiction titles for a book report assignment is a _____ request.
       (Skill 7.6) Rigorous

a.   ready reference
b.   research
c.   specific needs
d.   complex search

Answer: c. specific needs.

Requests made for particular titles or resources are known as special needs requests.Option C is the most appropriate answer.

33. **Which periodical contains book reviews of currently published children and young adult books?**
    (Skill 7.7) Rigorous

a. *Phi Delta Kappan*
b. *School Library Journal*
c. *School Library Media Quarterly*
d. *American Teacher*

Answer: b. School Library Journal

The *School Library Journal* is the world's largest book review source making Option B the best answer. *Phi Delta Kappan* is a professional journal for education. *School Library Media Quarterly* is a journal published by the American Library Association to assist with program administration of school library media programs. *American Teacher* is a magazine for the teaching profession.

34. **Recognition of children's book authors and illustrators is presented by:**
    (Skill 8.1) Easy

a. the FAME intellectual freedom committee.
b. the Sunshine State Book awards.
c. the Pineapple Press.
d. the DOE division of media services.

Answer: b. the Sunshine State Book awards.

Through the Sunshine State Book Awards, students in grades 3-5 evaluate and vote for one of fifteen titles to determine the award winner.

35. **The award given for the best children's literature (text) is:**
(Skill 8.1) Easy

a. the Caldecott.
b. the Newbery.
c. the Pulitzer.
d. the Booklist.

Answer: b. the Newbery

Option B, the Newbery Award, is the award given to an outstanding children's book. It was named for bookseller John Newbery, who was the first to publish literature for children in the second half of 18th century England. While the Caldecott Award does recognize children's literature, this award is for outstanding illustrators.

36. **Which writer composes young adult literature in the fantasy genre?**
(Skill 8.2) Rigorous

a. Stephen King
b. Piers Anthony
c. Virginia Hamilton
d. Phyllis Whitney

Answer: b. Piers Anthony

Piers Anthony is the author of such books as *Ghost, Firefly* and *Bio of an Ogre*. He is the only author listed that writes fantasy for young adults.

37. **Which fiction genre do authors Isaac Asimov, Louise Lawrence, and Andre Norton represent?**
(Skill 8.2) Rigorous

a. adventure
b. romance
c. science fiction
d. fantasy

Answer: c. science fiction

All of these authors represent Option C, science fiction titles for each include:
- Asimov's *I Robot* and *Foundation Trilogy*
- Lawrence's *Children of the Dust* and *Moonwind*
- Norton's *Stargate* and *Android at Arms*

38. **All of the following are authors of young adult fiction EXCEPT:**
(Skill 8.2) Rigorous

a. Paul Zindel.
b. Norma Fox Mazer.
c. S.E. Hinton.
d. Maurice Sendak.

Answer: d. Maurice Sendak

Maurice Sendak is best know for his picture books for young children such as *Where the Wild Things Are.*

39. **All of the following are authors of fantasy except:**
(Skill 8.2) Rigorous

a. Ray Bradbury.
b. Ursula LeGuin.
c. Piers Anthony.
d. Ann McCaffrey.

Answer: a. Ray Bradbury.

The most appropriate answer is A. Ray Bradbury is a science fiction author and the others are fantasy writers.

40. **The Caldecott Book Award was given to which book in 2002?**
(Skill 8.3) Rigorous

a. *The Three Pigs* by David Wiesner
b. *Had a Little Overcoat* Simms Taback
c. *Golem* by David Wisniewski
d. *Officer Buckle and Gloria* by Peggy Rathmann

Answer: **a** *The Three Pigs* by David Wiesner

The correct answer is Option A. *Had a Little Overcoat* is the 2000 winner. *Golem* is the 1997 winner. *Officer Buckle and Gloria* is the 1996 winner.

41.   **When selecting materials for a school library media collection which of the following must be considered?**
       (Skill 8.4) Easy

a.   cultural and ethical needs
b.   social value
c.   intellectual value
d.   all of the above

Answer: d. all of the above

When considering resources for a media center collection it is necessary to select materials that meet the cultural, ethical, social, and intellectual needs of the population it serves.

42.   **An online database that provides print and electronic journal subscriptions is:**
       (Skill 8.5) Rigorous

a.   Kids Connect.
b.   KQWeb.
c.   EBSCO.
d.   NICEM.

Answer: c. EBSCO

Option C, EBSCO is the most appropriate answer. It is an online database that provides print and electronic journals.

43.   **All of the following are periodical directories except:**
       (Skill 8.6) Average rigor

a.   *Ulrich's.*
b.   *TNYT.*
c.   *SIRS.*
d.   *PAIS.*

Answer: b. TNYT.
Option B is the most appropriate answer. All of the other are directories listed are specifically for periodicals.

44. A statement defining the core principles of a school library media program is called the:
(Skill 9.1) Average rigor

a. mission.
b. policy.
c. procedure.
d. objective.

Answer: a. mission

The core principles of an organization are outlined in a mission statement. An objective is a specific statement of measurable result that reflects the mission statement.

45. A general statement or outcome that is broken down into specific skills is known as:
(Skill 9.1) Average rigor

a. a policy.
b. a procedure.
c. a goal.
d. an objective.

Answer: c. goal

A goal is a general statement or outcome that is broken down into specific measurable objectives. Option C is the most appropriate answer.

46.   **Long range plans should span how many years?**
       (Skill 9.3) Easy

a.   2 – 4
b.   3 – 5
c.   5 – 10
d.   10 – 15

Answer: b. 3-5

Long range plans should be developed to span from 3-5 years. It is important to record progress and plan periodic evaluations to determine which goals may need to be adjusted due to changing student populations and funding.

47.   **Which of the following is characteristic of a short-range plan?**
       (Skill 9.4) Average rigor

a.   Accomplishable in three or more years
b.   Adheres to a rigid set of objectives
c.   Identifies immediate cost and funding sources
d.   Contains an abstract list of goals

Answer: c. Identifies immediate cost and funding sources

A short range plan typically spans one year or less, is flexible, is focused on a particular goal, and identifies cost and funding sources. This makes Option C the most appropriate answer.

48.   **The role of the Media Committee or Media Advisory Committee is to assist with all of the following except:**
       (Skill 9.5) Average rigor

a.   determine program direction.
b.   evaluate the media specialist.
c.   direct budget decisions.
d.   collaborate with the media specialist.

Answer: b. evaluate the media specialist

The Media Advisory Committee has the responsibility of helping to determine essential elements of the media collection, but they do not evaluate the media specialist.

49. **As a member of the school's curriculum team, the library media specialist's role would include all of the following except:**
    (Skill 9.6) Rigorous

a. ensuring a systematic approach to integrating information skills instruction.
b. advising staff on appropriate learning styles to meet specific objectives.
c. advising staff of current trends in curriculum design.
d. advising staff of objectives designed for specific content areas.

Answer: d. advising staff of objectives designed for specific content areas.

The school library media specialist can lend his or her expertise in the area of information skills integration, learning styles, and current trends in curriculum design. It is best to let the content area teachers plan for their specific objectives and the media specialist serve as a support person as listed previously.

50. **Which of the following is an example of quantitative data that would be used to evaluate a school library media program?**
    (Skill 1.2) Average rigor

a. Personnel evaluations
b. Usage statistics
c. Surveys
d. Interviews

Answer b. Usage statistics

Option B is the most appropriate answer because it is the only one listed that provides measurable data. All of the others are qualitative forms of data.

51.   An accredited elementary school has maintained an acceptable
       number of items in its print collection for ten years. In the evaluation
       review, this fact is evidence of both:
       (Skill 10.1) Rigorous

a.   diagnostic and projective standards.
b.   diagnostic and quantitative standards.
c.   projective and quantitative standards.
d.   projective and qualitative standards.

Answer: b. diagnostic and quantitative standards.

Diagnostic evaluations are standards based on conditions existing in programs
that have already been judged excellent. The acceptable print collection can be
compared to national guidelines for diagnostic information. Quantitative
evaluations involve numerical data of some kind. By taking a look at the
numbers in the collection the media specialist can review collection totals.
Option B is the correct answer.

52.   In preparation for submitting the media program's budget to the
       proper administrators, a media specialist should include all of the
       following except:
       (Skill 10.2) Rigorous

a.   Inventory logs to inform of lost, stolen, or damaged materials.
b.   List of books borrowed by the valedictorian to display types of materials
      that lead to successful performance at school.
c.   Class scheduling logs to show frequency of integration of classroom
      studies with the library media program.
d.   None of the above

**Answer: B. List of books borrowed by the valedictorian to display types of
materials that lead to successful performance at school.**

Sharing the records of an individual student would violate privacy rights.

53. **Ongoing evaluation is necessary to produce a quality media program. Which of the following can evaluation be used for?**
    (Skill 10.3) Rigorous

a. lobbying for budgetary or personnel support
b. to make changes to the use of the media center materials
c. to determine circulation regulations
d. all of the above

Answer: d. all of the above

Evaluating a media program can be very beneficial. It can assist the media specialist in justifying budget requests, making changes to the media center resources, and determine circulation regulations. Option D is the most appropriate answer.

54. **In formulating an estimated collection budget consider all of the following except:**
    (Skill 11.1) Rigorous

a. attrition by loss, damage, or age.
b. the maximum cost of item replacement.
c. the number of students served.
d. the need for expansion to meet minimum guidelines.

Answer: b. the maximum cost of item replacement

The first consideration for formulating a collection budget is to determine whether or not the collection meets minimum guidelines. Then, the media specialist should decide upon the funding needed to meet the guidelines. It is also important to allot funds to replace lost or worn items. Option B, the maximum cost of item replacement is not used in formulating a collection budget, thus making it the most appropriate answer.

55. **The most appropriate means of obtaining extra funds for library media programs is:**
(Skill 11.2) Average rigor

a.   having candy sales.
b.   conducting book fairs.
c.   charging fines.
d.   soliciting donations.

Answer: b. conducting book fairs.

The most appropriate answer for this question is Option B, conducting book fairs. This keeps in line with the main focus of a school library media program, literacy.

56. **To communicate budgetary needs and concerns, the best option for the media specialist is to:**
(Skill 11.3) Rigorous

a.   send memos to staff.
b.   determine needs based upon their own observations.
c.   work closely with the media advisory committee.
d.   none of the above

Answer: c. work closely with the media advisory committee

When communicating budgetary needs and concerns, the media specialist may need to send memos and create his or her own list. The best choice for this question is Option C. It is critical for the media specialist to work closely with the media advisory committee regarding all aspects of the media program, including the budget.

57. **In a school with one full-time library media assistant (clerk), which of the following are responsibilities of the assistant?**
(Skill 12.1) Average rigor

a.   selecting and ordering titles for the print collection
b.   performing circulation tasks and processing new materials
c.   inservicing teachers on the integration of media materials into the school curriculum
d.   planning and implementing programs to involve parents and community

Answer: b. performing circulation tasks and processing new materials.

Option B is the most appropriate answer. Circulation tasks and the processing of materials generally involve clerical duties. The other options are usually performed by licensed media specialists.

58. **Which of the following tasks should a volunteer NOT be asked to perform?**
    (Skill 12.1) Average rigor

a. decorating bulletin boards
b. demonstrating use of retrieval systems
c. maintaining bookkeeping records
d. fundraising

Answer: c. maintaining bookkeeping records

Volunteers are crucial to the effective running of a school library media center. Their assistance is invaluable in the areas of clerical tasks, creative tasks, and promoting the media center. However, the media specialist should be responsible for maintaining bookkeeping records to ensure the budgets are managed well, thus making Option C the most appropriate answer.

59. **AASL/AECT guidelines recommend that student library aides be:**
    (Skill 12.1) Average rigor

a. rewarded with grades or certificates for their service.
b. allowed to assist only during free time.
c. allowed to perform para- professional duties.
d. assigned tasks that relate to maintaining the atmosphere of the media center.

Answer: a. rewarded with grades or certificates for their service.

It is important to recognize students for the valuable service they perform as student library aides. In younger grades that recognition can come in the form or certificates. High school or middle school students may be a library aide as part of their course requirements. In this case, outstanding performance would be recognized in the form of grades. Option A is the most appropriate answer.

60. **A school with 500 – 749 students should have how many media specialists?**
(Skill 12.2) Easy

a.   1 part-time media specialist
b.   1 full time media specialist
c.   2 full time media specialist
d.   no media specialist required

Answer: b. 1 full time media specialist

It is recommended that schools with 500 to 749 students have at least 1 full time media specialist. This makes Option B the most appropriate response.

61. **The most efficient method of evaluating support staff is to**
(Skill 12.3) Average rigor

a.   administer a written test.
b.   survey faculty whom they serve.
c.   observe their performance.
d.   obtain verbal confirmation during   an employee interview.

Answer: c. observe their performance

The most efficient method of evaluating support staff is to observe their performance. An observation can provide an overall picture of the tasks they routinely perform. Observations may be conducted by the media specialist alone or in conjunction with another school administrator or fellow media specialist.

62. **Which of the following is a library policy, not a procedure?**
(Skill 13.1) Rigorous

a.   providing a vehicle for the circulation of audio-visual equipment.
b.   setting guidelines for collection development.
c.   determining the method for introducing an objective into the school improvement plan.
d.   setting categorical limits on operating expenses.

Answer: b. setting guidelines for collection development.

A policy is a plan or a course of action such as setting the guidelines for collection development, as listed in Option B. A procedure is a set of specific steps or methods used to perform a specific action.

63.   A policy is:
        (Skill 13.1) Easy

a.   a course of action taken to execute a plan.
b.   a written statement of principle used to guarantee a management practice.
c.   a statement of core values of an organization.
d.   a regulation concerning certification.

Answer: b. a written statement of principle used to guarantee a management practice.

The most appropriate answer is Option B. A policy is a written statement of principle used to guarantee a management practice. A mission is a statement of core values.

64.   **Collection development policies are developed to accomplish all of the following except**
        (Skill 13.2) Rigorous

a.   guarantee users freedom to access information.
b.   recognize the needs and interests of users.
c.   coordinate selection criteria and budget concerns.
d.   recognize rights of individuals or groups to challenge these policies.

Answer: c. coordinate selection criteria and budget concerns

The main goal of a collection development policy is to set guidelines and procedures that govern how resources are purchased and managed. It does not coordinate any criteria or address funding issues.

65.   **Which of the following should participate in the development of local policies and procedures?**
        (Skill 13.3) Average rigor

a.   teacher
b.   student
c.   parents
d.   all of the above

Answer: d. all of the above

Teachers, students and parents should play a role in the development of local policies and procedures. This ensures equity for all types of users by gaining insight from differing viewpoints. Administrators and media specialists should also serve on such a committee.

ED. MEDIA SPECIALIST PK-12   174

66. **A library procedures manual should contain which of the following?**
(Skill 13.4) Average rigor

a. mission
b. specific media policies
c. specific media procedures
d. all of the above

Answer: d. all of the above

A library procedures manual should contain the mission statement for the media program, policies (including collection development, acceptable use, circulation, etc.) and procedures for various tasks. Option D is the most appropriate answer.

67. **Current trends in school library media include all of the following except:**
(Skill 13.5) Average rigor

a. collaboration.
b. face to face instruction.
c. flexible scheduling.
d. technology integration.

Answer: b. face to face instruction.

Face to face instruction is not one of the current trends in school library media. Collaboration, flexible scheduling, and technology integration are some of the trends affecting school library media programs.

68. **Contemporary library media design models should consider which of the following an optional need?**
(Skill 14.1) Rigorous

a. flexibility of space to allow for reading, viewing, and listening.
b. space for large group activities such as district meetings, standardized testing, and lectures.
c. traffic flow patterns for entrance and exit from the media center as well as easy movement within the center.
d. adequate and easy to rearrange storage areas for the variety of media formats and packaging style of modern materials.

Answer: b. space for large group activities such as district meetings, standardized testing, and lectures.

Flexibility of space, traffic flow patterns that allow ease of movement, and adequate storage are all crucial to design of a media center. Therefore, Option B is the best answer. While a space for large group activities is desirable for community use, it is not vital to the operation of a school library media center.

69. **The most important consideration in the design of a new school library media center is:**
(Skill 14.1) Average rigor

a. the goals of the library media center program.
b. the location of the facility on the school campus.
c. state standards for facilities use.
d. the demands of current technologies.

Answer: a. the goals of the library media center program

The goals of a library media program should be a most important consideration when planning a new school media center. The other options should be considered, but Option A is the most appropriate answer.

70. **Factors that influence the atmosphere of a library media center contain all of the following except:**
    (Skill 14.2) Rigorous

    a. aesthetic appearance.
    b. acoustical ceiling and floor coverings.
    c. size of the media center.
    d. proximity to classrooms.

Answer: c. size of the media center

While the size of the media center is important, it does not necessarily have a bearing on the atmosphere. This makes Option C the most appropriate answer.

71. **MARC is the acronym for:**
    (Skill 15.1) Average Rigor

    a. Mobile Accessible Recorded Content
    b. Machine Accessible Readable Content
    c. Machine Readable Content
    d. Mobile Accessible Readable Content

Answer: c. Machine Readable Content

Option C is the most appropriate answer. MARC is the acronym for Machine Readable Content. The MARC format is used in the cataloging of resources.

72. **In which bibliographic field should information concerning the format of an audio-visual material appear?**
    (Skill 15.2) Rigorous

    a. Material specific details.
    b. Physical description.
    c. Notes.
    d. Standard numbers.

Answer: c. Notes

Using the 500 – General Note field in a MARC record, the format of the audio-visual materials can be listed. This makes Option C the most appropriate answer. The physical description contains information about the price and number of pages

73. **In what area of a bibliographic record can the name of the author be found?**
    (Skill 15.2) Average rigor

a. physical description area
b. publication area
c. terms of availability area
d. title and statement of responsibility area

Answer: d. title and statement of responsibility area.

The title and statement of responsibility area lists the title of the work, author, illustrator, and other pertinent information.

74. **Which of the following is not a component of a bibliographic record?**
    (Skill 15.2) Rigorous

a. Notes
b. Call number
c. Cover image
d. Physical description area

Answer: c. cover image

The cover image would be a detail listed under one of the components in a bibliographic record. It is not a component itself, making Option C the most appropriate response.

75. **OCLC is the acronym for:**
    (Skill 15.3) Average rigor

a. Online Computer Library Center
b. Online Computer Library Catalog
c. Online Computer Library Conference
d. Online Computer Library Content

Answer: a. Online Computer Library Center

The most appropriate answer is Option A, the Online Computer Library Center. This center provides bibliographic (MARC) records.

76. **AACR2 is the acronym for:**
    (Skill 15.3) Easy

a. Anglo-American Cataloging Rules Second Edition
b. American Association of Cataloging Rules Second Edition
c. American Association of Content Rules Second Edition
d. Anglo-American Content Rules Second Edition

Answer: a. Anglo-American Cataloging Rules Second Edition

Option A is the most appropriate answer. AACR2 outlines specific rules that must be followed when cataloging items.

77. **In MARC records the title information can be found under which tag?**
    (Skill 15.4) Rigorous

a. 130
b. 245
c. 425
d. 520

Answer: b. 245

The 245 tag is where the title information is recorded in a MARC record. Option B is the most appropriate response. The 520 tag is where the summary is listed.

78. **Following a standard set of international rules, *Anglo-American Cataloguing Rules*, enables users to locate materials equally well in all libraries that subscribe to these rules. To maintain this integrity, it is necessary for catalogers to do all of the following except:**
    (Skill 15.4) Rigorous

a. Recognize an International Standard Bibliographic Description (ISBD) that establishes the order in which bibliographic elements will appear in catalog entries.
b. Note changes that occur after each five years review of ISBD.
c. Agree to catalog all materials using the AACR standards.
d. Note changes that occur after each five year review of AACR.

Answer: d. Note changes that occur after each five year review of AACR.

Besides Option D, all of the following are necessary steps that catalogers must take to ensure integrity of records. This makes Option D the most appropriate answer.

79. The most efficient method of assessing which students are users or non-users of the library media center is reviewing:
    (Skill 16.1) Average rigor

    a.   patron circulation records.
    b.   needs assessment surveys of students.
    c.   monthly circulation statistics.
    d.   the accession book for the current year.

Answer: a. patron circulation records.

By reviewing circulation records the school library media specialists can quickly survey who is and isn't checking out materials making Option A the best answer. A needs assessment generally takes a good deal of time to complete. The monthly circulation records provide a snapshot of the number of books checked out during a specific period.

80. Libraries have changed from the stuffy no-talking zones of the past to bright, interactive, and frequently noisy epicenters of information at the heart of many schools. Which scenario best describes such a place?
    (Skill 16.2) Rigorous

    a.   The media specialist collaborates with teachers to integrate information skills into the curriculum.
    b.   In lieu of tables, cubicles are set up throughout the media center for students to work without disturbance.
    c.   When in need of assistance, teachers must submit a formal request to the media specialist.
    d.   The media center has set it's hours of operation to that of the school day. It is not open for early morning or after school usage.

Answer: a. The media specialist collaborates with teachers to integrate information skills into the curriculum.

The most appropriate answer is Option A. For a media program to be successful, the media specialist must work closely with classroom teachers to integrate information skills and technology into the curriculum. The media center should be an open space for collaboration. Cubicles in small numbers may be present, but they hamper the idea of group learning. The media specialist should be flexible and open to working with teachers and students as needed. While there may be a formal request for certain activities, it should not be the practice for all communication.

81. **Which of the following are examples of ways to promote the school library media programs?**
    (Skill 16.3) Easy

a. Attend school board meetings
b. Serve on the school's curriculum committee
c. Invite school board members to media planning meetings
d. All of the above

Answer: d. All of the above

Option D is the most appropriate answer. To promote the school library media program it is important that the media specialist attend school board meetings, serve on the school's curriculum committee, and invite school board members and other officials to media planning meetings.

82. **Which of the following is NOT one of three general criteria for selection of all materials?**
    (Skill 17.1) Average rigor

a. authenticity
b. appeal
c. appropriateness
d. allocation

Answer: d. allocation

When selecting materials the school library generally looks for materials that have reliable information, appeal to students and are appropriate for the grade levels its program serves. As Option D, allocation is not one of the criteria used to select materials

83. **Collection development principles in *Florida School Media Programs: A Guide for Excellence* recommend that: (Skill 17.2) Average rigor**

a.   only materials housed in the media center should be catalogued.
b.   only materials purchased with media center funds should be catalogued.
c.   all school-owned media resources should be catalogued in the media collection.
d.   materials already held in the district media catalog should not be purchased.

Answer: c. all school-owned media resources should be catalogued in the media collection

All resources owned by the school should be catalogued in the media collection, making Option C the most appropriate answer. By cataloging the resources the materials become part of the school inventory.

84. **Policies that determine procedures for copyright laws and reproduction of materials are generally determined at which level? (Skill 17.3) Average rigor**

a.   grade level
b.   school level
c.   community level
d.   district level

Answer: d. district level

Policies regarding copyright and acceptable use of resources are generally created at the district level. Individual schools may adopt extra requirements, but the overall guidelines are set on a larger scale.

85. **When determining a specific piece of equipment to purchase, the school library media specialist should first consult:**
(Skill 17.4) Average rigor

a. local vendors for a demonstration.
b. reviews in technology periodicals.
c. manufacturers' catalogs for specifications.
d. the state bid list for price.

Answer: c. manufacturer's catalogs for specifications.

Before purchasing a piece of equipment it is important to determine whether a particular piece will perform the needed task. One of the best places to find this answer is Option C, manufacturer's catalogs. The other resources may be helpful once the basic specifications have been checked.

86. **When selecting print or non-print materials all of the following are potential sources of current information except:**
(Skill 17.5) Easy

a. catalogs from publishers and vendors.
b. lists of award winners.
c. professional journals.
d. Internet search results.

Answer: d. an Internet search

It is best to select resources that come from reputable sources. An Internet search may bring results from any number of sources that may or may not be credible. Option D is the most appropriate answer.

87. **Books with strong picture support, familiar language patterns, and use of cuing systems are best for which group of students?**
(Skill 17.6) Average rigor

a. K-2
b. 3-5
c. 6-8
d. 9-12

Answer: a. K-2

The best answer is Option A. Young readers need books that have strong picture support, repetitive language patterns, and strong cuing systems.

88.	Which of these publications does not contain reviews for various types of publications?
	(Skill 2.2) Average rigor

a.	School Library Journal
b.	Booklist
c.	Media Center Review
d.	The Horn Book

Answer: c. Media Center Review

The best answer is c, Media Center Review. All of the other publications provide reviews for books and other resources.

89.	Comparing holdings records to bibliographies, conducting user surveys and examining resources are all procedures that may provide data for a:
	(Skill 17.7) Average rigor

a.	circulation evaluation.
b.	collection evaluation.
c.	program evaluation.
d.	school evaluation.

Answer: b. collection evaluation

All of the procedures listed can provide data for a collection evaluation. This makes Option B the most appropriate answer.

90.	The practice of examining the quantity and quality of the school library media resource collection which provides a "snapshot" of the collection is called:
	(Skill 17.7) Easy

a.	collection development.
b.	collection maintenance.
c.	collection mapping.
d.	weeding.

Answer: c. collection mapping.

Collection maps are of great benefit to the school library media specialist. They help to identify strengths and weaknesses in the collection, plan for purchases and identify areas in need of weeding. Option C is the most appropriate answer.

91.   Circulation limitations include:
        (Skill 18.1) Average rigor

a.   the number of items circulable to an individual borrower.
b.   the need for theft detection devices.
c.   overnight loans for special items.
d.   limits on circulation of reserve collections.

Answer: b. the need for detection devices.

Detection devices play a role in securing items but not in circulation limitations. Option B is the most appropriate answer.

92.   **When automating a library catalog it is important to consider which of the following prior to set up?**
        (Skill 18.2)

a.   technical requirements
b.   loan period
c.   patron limitations
d.   color of spine labels

Answer: a. technical requirements

Prior to establishing or upgrading an automated library catalog one of the most important considerations should be the technical requirements. Schools should examine their network infrastructure and individual computers to determine if the network will support the systems.

93.   **The procedures for conducting an inventory of the media collection include all of the following except:**
        (Skill 18.3) Rigorous

a.   Determining the cost of the inventory.
b.   Determining when the inventory will be conducted.
c.   Determining who will conduct the inventory.
d.   Determining if each item matches the information in the holding records.

Answer: a. Determine the cost of the inventory.

When conducting an inventory it is not necessary to determine the cost of the inventory. Option A is the most appropriate answer.

94. **To ensure the collection meets student needs which steps should the media specialist take?**
    (Skill 18.4) Rigorous

    a.   Develop specific processes for evaluating and updating the collection.

    b.   Have access to up-to-date collection monitoring and evaluation tools and reviewing resources.

    c.   Ensure that the media collection adheres to similar bibliographic lists.

    d.   Support the circulation of resources by sharing information with teachers and allowing them to preview new resources as well as take part in the selection process.

Answer: c. Ensure that the media collection adheres to similar bibliographic lists.

Option C is the most appropriate answer. It is the only option that is not considered a step to ensure the media collection meets student needs.

95. **The process of discarding worn or outdated books and materials is known as:**
    (Skill 18.5) Easy

    a.   weeding
    b.   inventory
    c.   collection mapping
    d.   eliminating

Answer: a. weeding

Option A is the most appropriate answer. Outdated or worn books and materials need to be removed from the library collection. This process is known as weeding.

96.	**Which of these Dewey Decimal classifications should be weeded most often?**
	(Skill 18.5) Rigorous

a.	100s
b.	500s
c.	700s
d.	Biographies

Answer: b. 500s

Materials in this section need to be continuously checked to ensure that the scientific information is correct. The 100s should be weeded every five to eight years. The 700s should be kept until worn, and the most current versions of biographies should be kept.

97.	**An acronym that is often used to remind media specialists of the steps to weeding a collection is:**
	(Skill 18.5) Average rigor

a.	WEAR
b.	MUSTIE
c.	ABCD
d.	RIPPED

Answer: b. MUSTIE

The acronym, MUSTIE, is used to assist media specialists with the weeding process. It stands for: Misleading, Ugly, Superseded, Trivial, Irrelevant, Elsewhere. This makes Option B the most appropriate answer.

98.	**Collaborative partnerships with staff can take on many forms. All of the following are examples except:**
	(Skill 19.1) Rigorous

a.	serving on curriculum development committees.
b.	viewing the school's curriculum and creating lessons.
c.	assisting teachers in planning, designing, and teaching lessons.
d.	assisting teachers and students with the use of new technologies.

Answer: b. viewing the school's curriculum and creating lessons

For the collaborative process to be effective the media specialist needs to work closely with the classroom teacher to create and plan lessons. The planning should not be conducted by the media specialist alone. This may occur, but it is not the desired result. Option B is the most appropriate answer.

99. **A good leader should:**
    (Skill 19.2) Average rigor

a. delegate responsibility.
b. show respect for colleagues.
c. engage in continuing education.
d. all of the above.

Answer: d. all of the above

Good leaders should strive to continuously improve their performance while building a great team to accomplish the desired goal. It is important that they demonstrate their quest to be lifelong learners, respect their colleagues, and learn to delegate responsibilities based upon the strengths of those around them.

100. **To foster the collaborative process the media specialist must possess all of the following skills except:**
     (Skill 19.3) Easy

a. leadership.
b. flexibility.
c. perversion.
d. persistence.

Answer: c. perversion.

A school library media specialist must possess flexibility, good leadership skills, and persistance, thus making Option C the most appropriate response.

101. **Florida State Law 231.15 identifies a school library media specialist as:**
     (Skill 20.1) Rigorous

a. a licensed support person.
b. an instructional employee.
c. a non-instructional employee.
d. an administrator/supervisor.

Answer: b. an instructional employee

Option B is the most appropriate response. According to Florida State Law 231.15 all teachers, library media specialists, principals, etc. are considered instructional employees.

102. The federal law enacted by Congress in December 2000 that imposed specific Internet restrictions on schools that receive Federal E-rate funding is known as:
(Skill 20.2) Average rigor

a. CIP.
b. CIPA.
c. SIP.
d. AUP.

Answer: b. CIPA

The Children's Internet Protection Act (CIPA) specifies that schools or libraries receiving Federal E-rate funding must enact certain guidelines such as Internet filters and monitoring software.

103. Which of the following has made the greatest impact on school library media centers in the last decade?
(Skill 21.1) Average rigor

a. censorship
b. emerging technologies
c. learning style research
d. state funding reductions

Answer: b. emerging technologies.

Advancements in technology have made the biggest impact in school library media centers during the last decade. These technologies have automated circulation, expanded available resources, and connected various locations through networks.

104. **Which of the following is NOT an expert in child development?** *(Skill 21.2) Rigorous*

a. Lawrence Kohlberg
b. James Naisbitt
c. Jean Piaget
d. Erik Erikson

Answer: b. James Naisbitt

Kohlberg is the developer of Modes of Learning. Piaget is one of the most influential developmental psychologists. Erik Erikson is also a well-known developmental psychologist. James Naisbitt is an author in the field of future studies making him the only one involved in child development; thus, Option B the best answer.

105. **All of the following organizations serve school libraries except:** *(Skill 22.1) Average rigor*

a. AASL.
b. AECT.
c. ALCT.
d. ALA.

Answer: c. ALCT.

The American Association of School Librarians (AASL), The Association for Educational Communications and Technology (AECT), and the American Library Association (ALA) are all organizations that support and serve school libraries.

106. **Which version of *Information Power* was published in 1998?** *(Skill 22.2) Easy*

a. *Information Power: The Role of the School Library Media Program*
b. *Information Power: A Review of Research*
c. *Information Power: Guidelines for School Library Media Programs*
d. *Information Power: Building Partnerships for Learning*

Answer: d. *Information Power: Building Partnerships for Learning*

Option D is the version that was published in 1998. *Information Power: Guidelines for School Library Media Programs* was published in 1988.

107. According to *Information Power*, which of the following is NOT a responsibility of the school library media specialist?
(Skill 22.2) Rigorous

a.   maintaining and repairing equipment
b.   instructing educators and parents in the use of library media resources
c.   providing efficient retrieval systems for materials and equipment
d.   planning and implementing the library media center budget

Answer: a. maintaining and repairing equipment

While the school library media specialist is responsible for program administration and aiding with instruction, his or her responsibilities do not include maintaining and repairing equipment. This is generally the duty of an assistant or technician

108. Which of the following is the best description of the ALA recommendations for certification for a school library media specialist?
(Skill 22.3) Average rigor

a.   a bachelor's degree in any content area plus 30 hours of library/information science
b.   a master's degree from an accredited Educational Media program.
c.   a bachelor's degree in library/ information science and a master's degree in any field of education
d.   a master's degree from an accredited Library and Information Studies program

Answer: d. a master's degree from an accredited Library and Information Studies Program

According to the American Library Association, to become a certified school librarian one should attain a master's degree from an ALA accredited Library and Information Studies Program. It is important to check a program's accreditation status before pursuing a degree at that institution. Some locations will not hire librarians who did not graduate from accredited programs.

109. The **TAXONOMIES OF THE SCHOOL LIBRARY MEDIA PROGRAM** outlines eleven levels of school library media specialists' involvement with curriculum and instruction and was developed by: *(Skill 22.3) Rigorous*

a. Eisenberg.
b. Bloom.
c. Loertscher.
d. Lance.

Answer: c. Loertscher

Eisenberg is one of the creators of the Big 6 Model. Bloom was the developer of Bloom's Taxonomy. Keith Curry-Lance has conducted many studies on the effect of school library media programs on student achievement.

110. **The Right to Read Statement was issued by:** *(Skill 23.1) Rigorous*

a. AECT.
b. ALA.
c. NCTE.
d. NICEM.

Answer: c. NCTE

The National Council of Teachers of English (NCTE) is responsible for the creation of the Right to Read Statement. This make Option C the most appropriate answer.

111. **In the landmark U.S. Supreme Court ruling in favor of Pico, the court's opinion established that**
     (Skill 23.2) Rigorous

a.   library books, being optional not required reading, could not be arbitrarily removed by school boards.
b.   school boards have the same jurisdiction over library books as they have over textbooks.
c.   the intent to remove pervasively vulgar material is the same as the intent to deny free access to ideas.
d.   First Amendment challenges in regards to library books are the responsibility of appeals courts.

Answer: a. library books, being optional not required reading, could not be arbitrarily removed by school boards.

In *Board of Education, Island Trees Union Free School District No. 26 v. Pico* the Supreme Court states that library books, being optional, non-required reading, could not be arbitrarily removed by school boards

112. **When creating a schedule for a school library media center the type of schedule that maximizes access to resources is a:**
     (Skill 23.3) Easy

a.   fixed schedule.
b.   open schedule.
c.   partial fixed schedule.
d.   flexible schedule.

Answer: d. flexible schedule.

The best answer is d, flexible schedule. A flexible schedule allows students to have access to resources at the point of need. It maximizes the use of resources and allows media specialists to be accessible for collaborative planning with teachers.

113. The school library media center should be an inviting space that encourages learning. To accomplish this, the school library media specialist should do all of the following except:
(Skill 23.3) Average rigor

a.   collaborate with school staff and students.
b.   create a schedule where each class comes to the media center each week for instruction.
c.   arrange materials so that they are easy to locate.
d.   promote the program as a wonderful place for learning.

Answer: b. create a schedule where each class comes to the media center each week for instruction

The goal of a school library is to operate under a flexible schedule to maximize use of the media center and its resources. This makes Option B the most appropriate answer.

114. The Position Statement on Flexible Scheduling was developed by:
(Skill 23.3) Average rigor

a.   AASL.
b.   ALA.
c.   AECT.
d.   SLMA.

Answer: a. AASL

The American Association of School Librarians has issued the Position Statement on Flexible Scheduling. It recommends full integration of information skills into the curriculum. Option A is the most appropriate answer.

115. All of the following are benefits of interlibrary loan except:
(Skill 23.4) Rigorous

a.   maximizing the use media center funds.
b.   providing a wider range of resources available for patrons.
c.   building partnerships with outside agencies.
d.   eliminating the need for media assistants.

Answer: d. eliminating the need for media assistants

The most appropriate response is Option D. Interlibrary loan allows the cooperating entities to maximize both funds and resources. It does not eliminate the need for media assistants.

116. **Instructional materials are evolving into all of the following formats except:**
(Skill 23.5) Average rigor

a. ebooks.
b. online magazines.
c. audio cassettes.
d. interactive software.

Answer: c. audio cassettes

Audio cassettes have given way to newer formats such as CD-ROMs and mp3 files. This makes Option C the most appropriate response.

117. **Which professional journal is published by the American Association of School Librarians?**
(Skill 24.1) Average rigor

a. *School Library Media Research*
b. *Library Trends*
c. *Library Power*
d. *Voices of Youth Advocate*

Answer: a. *School Library Media Research*

The only journal listed that is published by the AASL is *School Library Media Research*. This makes Option A the most appropriate response.

118. **When reviewing research information a media specialist should consider all of the following except: (Skill 24.2)**

a. What was the topic of the report?
b. How does the information found in this project fit what is known?
c. How was the research completed?
d. All of the above

Answer: d. All of the above

All are things to consider when reviewing research information. Option D is the most appropriate answer.

119. According to research on promotion techniques and support for library media programs, their staunchest ally must be the
(Skill 24.3) Rigorous

a.   teaching faculty.
b.   student body.
c.   district media supervisor.
d.   school principal.

Answer: d. school principal

In order to make the necessary changes needed to make the school library media center the true learning center of the school the school library media specialist must have the full support of the principal. Moving to flexible scheduling and truly integrated learning can be a big adjustment. It is only with the vision and leadership of the school principal that any changes can occur.

120. When a suspected infringement of copyright is brought to the attention of the school library media specialist, he or she should follow certain procedures. Which of the following is not one of the procedures?
(Skill 25.1) Rigorous

a.   If an instance is verified, tactfully inform the violator of the specific criteria to use so that future violations can be avoided. Presented properly, the information will be accepted as constructive.

b.   Determine if a violation has in effect occurred. Never accuse or report alleged instances to a higher authority without verification.

c.   If advice is unheeded and further infractions occur, bring them to the attention of the teacher's supervisor (e.g., a team leader or department chair) who can handle the matter as an evaluation procedure.

d.   If further infractions persist after the teacher's supervisor has been notified then it is necessary to consult the proper authorities to handle the situation.

Answer: d. If further infractions persist after the teacher's supervisor has been notified then it is necessary to consult the proper authorities to handle the situation.

Copyright infractions are generally handled on site and can be taken care of through the procedures listed in options A through C. Option D is the most appropriate answer.

121. When a parent complains about the content of a specific title in a library media collection, the library media specialist's first course of action in responding to the complaint is to
(Skill 25.2) Rigorous

a. remove the title from the shelf and purge it from both the catalog and the shelf list.
b. place the book in reserve status for circulation at parent request only.
c. submit the complaint to a district review committee.
d. explain the principles of intellectual freedom to the complaining parent.

Answer: d. explain the principles of intellectual freedom to the complaining parent.

Following the Library Bill of Rights and the principles of Intellectual Freedom, the primary mission of a school library media program is to provide access to information without censorship, therefore making Option D the best answer.

122. The responsibility for appointing a reconsideration committee to examine a challenged material belongs to
(Skill 25.2) Average rigor

a. the school superintendent.
b. the district media supervisor.
c. the school principal.
d. the school library media specialist.

Answer: b. the district media supervisor

The first levels of challenged materials are handled within the school first by the media specialist with the assistance of the principal. Once the challenge necessitates the formation of a committee, the responsibility falls upon the district media supervisor.

123. **A student looks for a specific title on domestic violence. When he learns it is overdue, he asks the library media specialist to tell him the borrower's name. The library media specialist should first**
(Skill 25.3) Rigorous

a.   readily reveal the borrower's name.
b.   suggest he look for the book in another library.
c.   offer to put the boy's name on reserve pending the book's return.
d.   offer to request an interlibrary loan.

Answer: c. offer to put the boy's name on reserve pending the book's return.

Patron confidentiality is of the utmost importance. The media specialist also needs to meet the needs of the patron requesting the book. The most appropriate course of action is Option C. The specialist should offer to put the boy's name on reserve pending the book's return.

124. **Which of the following is the least effective way of communicating school library media policies, procedures, and rules to media center patrons?**
(Skill 17.8) Average rigor

a.   announcements made in faculty and parent support group meetings
b.   a published faculty procedures manual
c.   written guidelines in the student handbook or special media handbill
d.   a videotape orientation viewed over the school's closed circuit television system

Answer: a. announcements made in faculty and parent support group meetings.

When providing information regarding policies, procedures and rules for media center patrons it is important to provide them with tangible and detailed information. With Option A, announcements at meetings, the information is not necessarily written down and the media specialist may have to rely on those present to share information with others.   It is the least reliable.

125. **Which of the following media should be included in the school library media center's resource collection?**
(Skill 17.4) Rigorous

a.   audio recordings
b.   periodicals
c.   online resources
d.   all of the above

Answer: d. all of the above

A school library media collection should contain a wide array of materials in various formats. Audio recordings, periodicals, and online resources should be a part of the collection, along with any other types of resources. This makes Option D the most appropriate answer.

XAMonline, INC. 21 Orient Ave. Melrose, MA 02176

Toll Free number 800-509-4128

TO ORDER Fax 781-662-9268 OR www.XAMonline.com

FLORIDA TEACHER CERTICATION EXAMINATIONS - FTCE - 2007

PO#   Store/School:

Bill to Address 1   Ship to address

City, State Zip

Credit card number_____-_____-_____-_____   expiration_____

EMAIL _____

PHONE   **FAX**

13# ISBN 2007	TITLE	Qty	Retail	Total
978-1-58197-900-8	Art Sample Test K-12			
978-1-58197-801-8	Biology 6-12			
978-1-58197-099-9	Chemistry 6-12			
978-1-58197-572-7	Earth/Space Science 6-12			
978-1-58197-578-9	Educational Media Specialist PK-12			
978-1-58197-908-4	Elementary Ed. Sample Questions			
978-1-58197-907-7	Elementary Education K-6			
978-1-58197-915-2	English 6-12			
978-1-58197-904-6	Exceptional Student Ed. K-12			
978-1-51897-905-3	Family and Consumer Science			
978-1-58197-906-0	FELE Florida Ed. Leadership			
978-1-58197-919-0	French Sample Test 6-12			
978-1-58197-902-2	General Knowledge			
978-1-58197-916-9	Guidance and Counseling PK-12			
978-1-58197-089-0	Humanities K-12			
978-1-58197-914-5	Mathematics 6-12			
978-1-58197-911-4	Middle Grades English 5-9			
978-1-58197-912-1	Middle Grades General Science 5-9			
978-1-58197-924-4	Middle Grades Integrated Curriculum			
978-1-58197-910-7	Middle Grades Math 5-9			
978-1-58197-913-8	Middle Grades Social Science 5-9			
978-1-58197-920-6	Physical Education K-12			
978-1-58197-818-6	Physics 6-12			
978-1-58197-903-9	Professional Educator			
978-1-58197-909-1	Reading K-12			
978-1-58197-917-6	Social Science 6-12			
978-1-58197-918-3	Spanish K-12			
			SUBTOTAL	
Add ship/handling $8.25 one title, $11.00 two titles, $15.00 three or more titles				
			TOTAL	

CPSIA information can be obtained at www.ICGtesting.com
Printed in the USA
BVOW050514160413

318285BV00005B/266/P